תרומה

Terumah

Shabbat Morning Edition

Elliott Michaelson

MAJS

Copyright Information

Classroom Essentials ◊ Textbooks & E-books ◊ Smartphone & Tablet Apps

Practical Solutions
for Jewish Education...
www.adventurejudaism.net

4"x3" playing cards are great for match games, fish, memory games, and more! Suggestions for games are included.

Build Your ALEF-BET
Full edition with vowels and endings!

A hands-on approach to mastering the Alef-Bet...

Hands-on learning with the Build Your Alef-Bet app, card sets, and textbooks!

A unique, hands-on approach to mastering the alef-bet — with built-in flexibility for any program! It's also a great resource for Special Ed. Available in two textbook editions: basic (letters only) and full (letters, vowels, and ending letters).

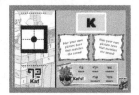

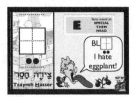

7"x5" flashcards are great for small groups, memory games, and more!

Smartphone / Tablet App!

Swipe, move and rotate line segments into place as you build each letter of the Hebrew alphabet. For Apple and Android.

Build Your Alef-Bet

PLAY
OPTIONS
HELP

11"x8" display cards are great for word walls, sorting games, class displays, and more!

Combine these other great products with Build Your Alef-Bet to enhance your learning experience!

The Wandering Jew Presents...

Ultimate
גימטריא
GEMATRIA
1 10 200 9 40 10 3

Great way to learn the numerical values of the Hebrew letters! 10"x7" display cards, 7"x5" flashcards, and 4"x3" playing cards.

HEBREW Punch-Out Letters

IDEAL FOR...
Bulletin Boards ◊ Class Projects ◊ Displays ◊ Announcements ◊ And much more!

Each set contains...

Also includes vowels, punctuation, and Torah trop!

◊ Long-lasting, durable, card stock!

◊ Bright colours!

◊ Reusable!

Actual Size & Type

Suggestions? Questions? Want to say "hi"? Visit us at: www.adventurejudaismessentials.com

© Adventure Judaism Classroom Solutions, Inc. Made in Canada.

A must-have for any Jewish program — just punch them out and pin them up! Perfect for bulletin boards, class projects, displays, announcements, alef-bet games and more. Choose from 8 vivid colours on varnished card stock.

PARASHAT TERUMAH

Vital Statistics

Full text reference:	*Shemot / Exodus 25: 1 to 27: 19*
The Maftir reading:	*Shemot / Exodus 27: 17-19*
Text reference for the Haftarah:	*1 Mela̱him / Kings 5: 26 to 6: 13*

Special Maftir and Haftarah for Shabbat Rosh H̲odesh

The Maftir reading:	*Ba-Midbar / Numbers 28: 9-15*
Text reference for the Haftarah:	*Yish'ayah / Isaiah 66: 1-24*

Special Maftir and Haftarah for Shabbat Za̱hor

The Maftir reading:	*Devarim / Deuteronomy 25: 17-19*
Text reference for the Haftarah:	*1 Shemu'el / Samuel 15: 1-34 (or 15: 2-34)*

Note: the English retelling of the Torah is for the entire Parashah, not just the Maftir. The English for the Maftir consists of the last parts of the retelling.

BEFORE YOU BEGIN: GOOD THINGS TO ASK ABOUT THIS BOOK

Welcome to your Bar/Bat Mitzvah Survival Guide! There are some unique features about this guide that might be useful to you during your studies, such as...

What's up with the names of people and places?

Brace yourself, for what I'm about to say (or write, actually) may come as a shock. THE TORAH IS WRITTEN IN HEBREW. Big surprise, I know. So here's the issue many of my students have: in English, we call him *Moses* but in the Torah, we call him *Moshe*. The first woman on Earth is called *Eve* but in Hebrew, she's called *Hava*. The Jews were slaves in *Egypt* — or was it *Mitzra'im*? The answer is both. To try to avoid this confusion between English and Hebrew names, I've decided to stick with the Hebrew. So מֹשֶׁה is translated as *Moshe*, not *Moses*, and יְרוּשָׁלַיִם is *Yerushalayim*, not *Jerusalem*. For more on how to pronounce the Hebrew names, check out the handy translation chart on page six.

How do you show God talking?

Many of us think of God as an inspirational force in our lives, but how many of us have actual physical conversations with God? As a kid, I was always confused by the fact that God physically speaks to people in the Torah but not to us today. When the Torah records God's "speech", we don't have to think of it as physical words all the time. Moses Maimonides was one of the greatest philosophers and teachers in Judaism, and 800 years ago he famously taught that all divine language in the Torah is metaphorical. Taking that to heart, I've done my very best to express that in my English retellings. God's "dialogue" is written in a different font and with a different tone, and I avoid using direct language like "said" or "told". So did Avraham hear the actual voice of God, or did God act as Avraham's inspirational inner voice? Both beliefs are valid, and it's something I encourage you to explore with your family and your teacher / rabbi.

In these retellings, I refer to God by two proper nouns: *Adonai* and *Elohim*. *Adonai* is God's actual, personal name: יְ-ה-ו-ה. You'll find it all over the place in the Tanah and in many *sidurim*. *Elohim* (אֱלֹהִים) is the Hebrew word for "God". Since the Tanah uses both as personal names for God, I've decided to keep the proper Hebrew terms.

What about commentary and translation?

Judaism has always accepted that the Torah text contains four layers of understanding. There's the literal, basic text that you see in front of you (*peshat*), but underneath the basic text are three layers of metaphorical understanding just waiting to be discovered (*derash, remez, sod*). You have over two thousand years of scholarship and commentary — including some great stuff being written today — to help you discover these hidden meanings. I've deliberately avoided providing them here for one all-important reason: any commentaries I select would reflect *my* perspective on the text and how it should be taught, and I want you to be free to find *your own way*. That's why I'm leaving the selection of commentary up to you and your rabbi / teacher.

Instead, I've devoted my time to a careful retelling of the Torah and Haftarah texts in English. This isn't a strict translation, but it isn't a sanitized children's version, either. My aim is to provide an English format that flows as easily as a work of juvenile literature, but which preserves the content and significance of the Biblical text. I've also included suggestions for study and analysis that are based on media literacy expectations from public school programs. These blurbs usually address social and historical questions that my own students ask because they need help understanding the ancient society that produced our sacred texts. None of this replaces Rabbinic commentary. To the contrary — once you understand a little bit about the world of our ancient cousins, you can work with your rabbi / teacher to find the commentaries that speak to your own interests and concerns.

Da Links!

If you're using the ebook version of this book, try tapping the hyperlinks that appear periodically in the text. Some of them will take you to useful Google maps of many of the locations mentioned in the Torah, while others will take you the *Jewish Virtual Library* or *My Jewish Learning* to learn more about the famous people and nations from the Torah and Haftarah. Enjoy!

TRANSLITERATIONS OF HEBREW VOWEL SOUNDS

(A very handy reference guide...)

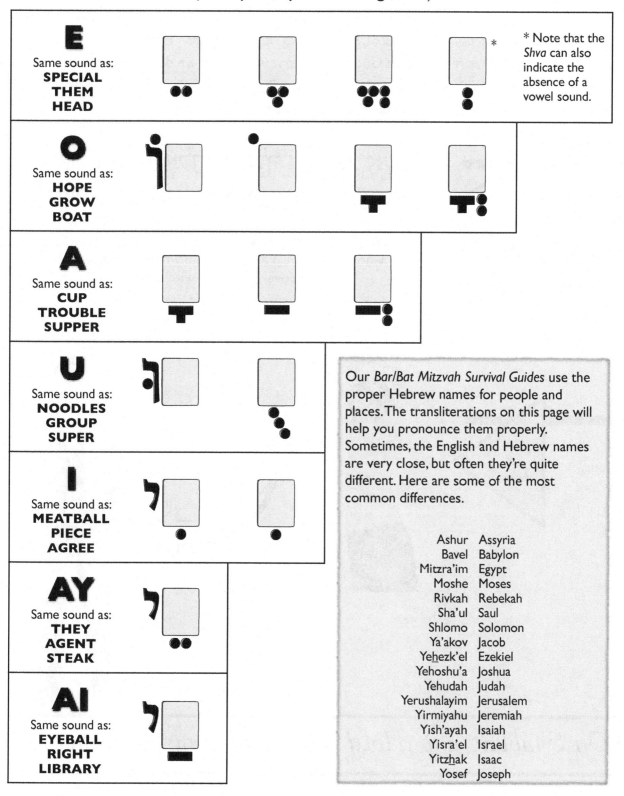

E

Same sound as:
**SPECIAL
THEM
HEAD**

* Note that the *Shva* can also indicate the absence of a vowel sound.

O

Same sound as:
**HOPE
GROW
BOAT**

A

Same sound as:
**CUP
TROUBLE
SUPPER**

U

Same sound as:
**NOODLES
GROUP
SUPER**

I

Same sound as:
**MEATBALL
PIECE
AGREE**

AY

Same sound as:
**THEY
AGENT
STEAK**

AI

Same sound as:
**EYEBALL
RIGHT
LIBRARY**

Our *Bar/Bat Mitzvah Survival Guides* use the proper Hebrew names for people and places. The transliterations on this page will help you pronounce them properly. Sometimes, the English and Hebrew names are very close, but often they're quite different. Here are some of the most common differences.

Ashur	Assyria
Bavel	Babylon
Mitzra'im	Egypt
Moshe	Moses
Rivkah	Rebekah
Sha'ul	Saul
Shlomo	Solomon
Ya'akov	Jacob
Yehezk'el	Ezekiel
Yehoshu'a	Joshua
Yehudah	Judah
Yerushalayim	Jerusalem
Yirmiyahu	Jeremiah
Yish'ayah	Isaiah
Yisra'el	Israel
Yitzhak	Isaac
Yosef	Joseph

PUTTING ON THE TALLIT & TEFILLIN

If you've never had the chance to put on the *tallit* or *tefillin*, this is your lucky day! Traditionally, the *tallit* and *tefillin* are worn for all weekday morning services. On Shabbat and Holy Day mornings, only the *tallit* is worn (except Yom Kippur, when we wear the tallit all day). Why the difference? There are many explanations. My favorite reason goes like this: the Torah teaches us to wear reminders of our Divine Agreement with God on our arms and our heads (i.e. *tefillin*). On Shabbat, Pesah, Shavu'ot, Sukkot, Rosh Hashanah, and Yom Kippur, we perform rituals all day long that remind us of God's Agreement with us, so we don't need the *tefillin* to remind us. To put everything on, follow these basic steps. You can also find a video on our website at **http://www.adventurejudaism.net/Bar_Bat_Mitzvah_Guides.html**.

1

Recite the bra<u>h</u>ah for wrapping yourself in the tallit.

בָּרוּךְ אַתָּה יְיָ אֱלֹהֵינוּ מֶלֶךְ הָעוֹלָם, אֲשֶׁר קִדְּשָׁנוּ בְּמִצְוֹתָיו, וְצִוָּנוּ לְהִתְעַטֵּף בַּצִּיצִת.

We praise You, Adonai our God, Ruler of the universe, whose *mitzvot* make us holy, and who commanded us to cover ourselves with *tzitzit*.

2

Wrap the collar around your shoulders as if you were putting on a cape.

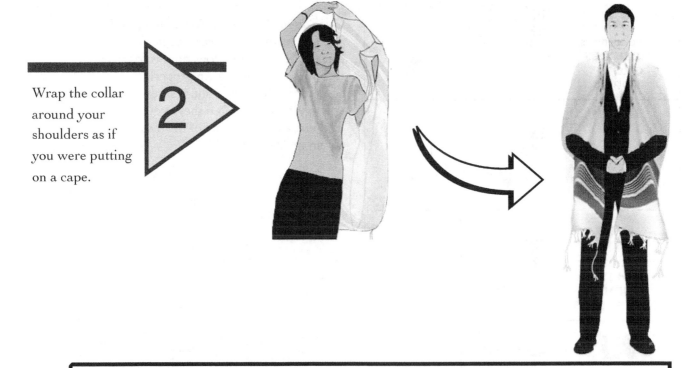

On Shabbat and Holy Day mornings, stop here!

3

Loop the *tefillin shel yad* (the one with the extra-long strap) around your bicep.

If you're left-handed, use your right bicep. If you're right-handed, use your left bicep. If you're ambidextrous like me, take your pick!

4

Before tightening the loop, recite this bra<u>h</u>ah.

בָּרוּךְ אַתָּה יְיָ אֱלֹהֵינוּ מֶלֶךְ הָעוֹלָם, אֲשֶׁר קִדְּשָׁנוּ בְּמִצְוֹתָיו, וְצִוָּנוּ לְהָנִיחַ תְּפִלִּין.

We praise You, Adonai our God, Ruler of the universe, whose *mitzvot* make us holy, and who commanded us to put on *tefillin*.

5

Tighten the loop around your bicep and wrap the strap around your forearm 7 times.

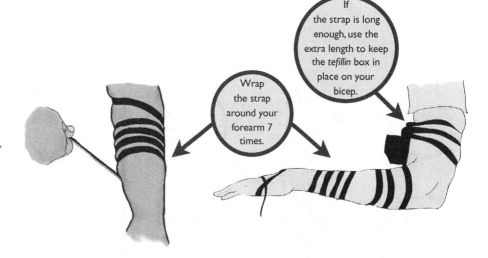

Wrap the strap around your forearm 7 times.

If the strap is long enough, use the extra length to keep the *tefillin* box in place on your bicep.

6

Place the *tefillin shel rosh* at the center of your forehead, right at the hairline.

Two long straps extend from the back of the *tefillin shel rosh*. Let them hang freely on either side of your head.

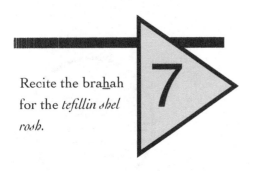

7

Recite the brahah for the *tefillin shel rosh*.

בָּרוּךְ אַתָּה יְיָ אֱלֹהֵינוּ מֶלֶךְ הָעוֹלָם, אֲשֶׁר קִדְּשָׁנוּ בְּמִצְוֹתָיו, וְצִוָּנוּ עַל מִצְוַת תְּפִלִּין.

We praise You, Adonai our God, Ruler of the universe, whose *mitzvot* make us holy, and who commanded the *mitzvah* of *tefillin*.

8

Finish wrapping the *tefillin shel yad* by winding it around your middle finger 3 times.

If the strap is long enough, you can also wind it around your hand to help keep everything in place.

Tefillin shel rosh with the two hanging straps.

Tefillin shel yad around the bicep (under the tallit.)

Tefillin shel yad wrapped 3 times around the middle finger.

Tefillin shel yad wrapped 7 times around the forearm.

You're ready to go! When you're finished, take everything off in the reverse order.

WEEKLY PARASHAH & HAFTARAH

SHEMOT / EXODUS 25: 1 TO 27: 19 IN ENGLISH

What's the story so far?

It's been three generations since the final events of the book of *Bereshit / Genesis*. The family that began with Avraham & Sarah, Yitzhak & Rivkah, and the twelve sons of Ya'akov, Le'ah & Rahel, has now grown into the twelve tribes of Benay Yisra'el. Having endured slavery in Mitzra'im (Egypt) and newfound liberation, the people of Benay Yisra'el are now camped at Mount Sinai as Moshe delivers the details of their Brit (divine agreement) with God.

What can I expect from this Parashah?

There are three main story arcs in the book of *Shemot / Exodus*. They are:

(1) Enslavement and rescue;

(2) Renewal of the Brit (divine agreement) between God and Benay Yisra'el;

(3) Origin of Benay Yisra'el's religious culture.

The Parashot *Terumah, Teztaveh, Ki Tisa, Va-Yakhel,* and *Pekuday* describe the origin of the religion of ancient Yisra'el, including the famous Golden Calf incident. Apart from this, the Torah has important concerns that are reflected in this Parashah:

• Revealing the origins of the people of Yisra'el;

• Demonstrating God's power;

• Highlighting God's special interest in the Jewish people and explaining why the Jewish people have a special interest in God.

And so, without further ado, on to the Torah...

Warning: Read this first!

Our Parashah is an important part of the origin story of the people of Yisra'el which takes up the entire book of *Shemot / Exodus*. To fully understand what's happening here, it helps to know how it connects to the themes before and after. *Shemot's* basic themes are shown below, with our Parashah in bold:

Enslavement of Benay Yisra'el → God appoints Moshe to lead the people to freedom → no-one takes Moshe seriously → God confirms Moshe's authority → the first seven plagues against Mitzra'im → the last three plagues → leaving Mitzra'im → escape at the Sea of Reeds → challenges of living in the wilderness → conflict with wilderness tribes → creating a political system → Brit at Sinai → accepting a code of civil law → **building a religious centre** → establishing religious leadership → religious rebellion → reiterating the Brit → constructing the Mishkan (God's "House") and everything in it → the Brit and God move into the Mishkan.

MANDATORY GIFTS

> **25: 1-9**
> The Weekday & Shabbat afternoon reading starts here.

A Message from Adonai came to Moshe.

Tell Benay Yisra'el to take a terumah for me from every person whose heart is willing. The terumot you shall take may be gold, silver, and copper; high quality blue, purple and crimson fabrics; high quality linen and goats' hair; animal hides from the ram (dyed red) and the tahash; wood from the acacia tree; olive oil for the lamp; spices for the anointing oil and incense; and precious gems and stones for the Efod and the Hoshen. They will make a Sacred Space for Me so I may live among them. They will assemble the Mishkan and its furnishings according to the designs I will show you.

Terumah: A תְּרוּמָה is a kind of "mandatory gift". This is an odd concept — how can a gift be mandatory? Is there anything we do today that may be technically voluntary, but which we feel is "mandatory" or "expected" of us? Discuss your ideas. Compare and contrast God's תְּרוּמָה with King Shlomo's mandatory "gifts" in the Haftarah.

The תְּרוּמָה we see here doesn't come cheap. These luxury items must have cost the community a lot. As you read through the Parashah, see if you can identify what these items were used for. How does this help you understand the idea of the תְּרוּמָה — a mandatory gift? Can you think of anything we do today that compares to this? Your rabbi / teacher can help you explore your ideas.

Tahash: This was a type of animal, but no-one is exactly sure which one. Translators have it as a badger, a seal, or even a dolphin. Because of this uncertainty, I've decided to use the original Hebrew word.

Efod: This was a mantle or a cape worn by the Kohanim (priests).

Hoshen: This was a ritual breastplate worn by the Kohen Ha-Gadol (High Priest). Twelve different semiprecious stones representing Yisra'el's tribes were set into it in two columns.

Mishkan: This was the portable shrine that housed Benay Yisra'el's holy objects. It was considered to be the Sacred Space where God "lived' among the people.

THE ARK OF THE COVENANT

25: 10-16
The Weekday and Shabbat afternoon reading ends at vs. 16.

They shall make the Aron out of acacia wood. It will be two and a half amot long, one and a half amot wide, and one and a half amot high. Coat it inside and out with gold and crown it with gold molding all around. Cast four gold rings and attach them to the Aron's legs (two rings on each side). Carve two poles out of acacia wood, coat them with gold, and slide them through the rings on either side. This is how you will carry the Aron. The do not remove the poles from the rings. Inside the Aron you will place the record of the Edut that I give to you.

Aron: The אֲרֹן was the large, ornate box that held the written records of God's mitzvot from Mount Sinai. What do synagogues use today in place of this Aron? Explore the differences and similarities.

Amot: The אַמָּה (plural, אַמּוֹת) was an ancient unit of measurement. It's usually translated as "cubit". It was the distance from elbow to fingertip, roughly eighteen inches or half a meter. So how big was the Aron in modern terms? I'll let you figure it out.

Edut: עֵדֻת is usually translated as "Testimony" or "Pact". It refers to the original record of God's Brit (Divine Agreement) with the Jewish people. The Brit outlines God's responsibilities to the Jewish people and the Jewish people's responsibilities to God. What are they? Check out the two previous parashot, *Yitro* and *Mishpatim*, for details.

Why was it necessary to build such a fancy and expensive box just to house a couple of stone tablets? Think about what these tablets represent. Is there anything that countries have today that might be the equivalent of the Edut? What about modern Jewish practice? Your rabbi / teacher can help you explore these ideas.

Keruv: This was a mythical winged creature with human and animal features. The Tanah isn't entirely clear as to exactly what Keruvim looked like, but our ancestors certainly knew. The top of the Aron was decorated with two golden Keruvim. They faced each other from opposite ends of the Aron and had their wings stretched out with the tips touching. God's Messages came to Moshe from between these two Keruvim.

25: 17-22

The lid will be made of pure gold. It will be two and a half amot long and one and a half amot wide. At either end, make a keruv out of beaten gold. The lid and the keruvim shall be of a single piece. Arrange them so that they face one another, with their wings spread forth to cover the top of the lid. Place the lid on top of the Aron, and within the Aron place the Edut I will give you.

This is where I will confer with you. Anything I command to Benay Yisra'el will come to you from between the two keruvim atop the Aron.

FANCY FURNISHING

25:23-30

God's Message to Moshe continued.

Use acacia wood for the ritual table. Make it two amot long, one amah wide, and one and a half amot high. Coat it completely with gold and crown it all around with gold molding. Add a rim one handspan high around the edge of the table and crown it with a golden molding. Cast four golden rings and attach one to each of the table's legs just below the molding. Carve two poles out of acacia wood, overlay them with gold, and slide them through the rings on either side. This is how you will carry the table.

*Cast out of pure gold the pans, bowls, ladles, and jars that will be used for **libations**. Loaves of **showbread** will be permanently displayed on the table.*

The Mishkan had three sections to it. The outermost part was the public area where the community gathered. This public area surrounded a small pavilion which was the Mikdash (God's Sacred Space). The back part of the Mikdash was the Kodesh Ha-Kodashim (Holy of Holies). The Aron was kept inside the Kodesh Ha-Kodashim. Everything else, including the ritual table, the Menorah, and the incense altar, were kept in the Mikdash.

Ritual table: This was an ornate table used by the kohanim for ceremonial gifts of water and food to God.

Libations...Showbread: A "libation" is an offering of water or a drink to a god, and it was a common practice in Ye Olden Dayes (it's still a common practice in many religions today). "Showbread" was actual bread that was put on display as part of a weekly ritual — twelve loaves that were *shown* to God for a week before being eaten by God's representatives (the kohanim) and then replaced by twelve fresh loaves. Why twelve? See if you can figure it out (hint: think about what you know about the tribes of Yisra'el).

In Ye Olden Dayes, it was common for priests to win their gods' favor by laying out ceremonial meals for the gods to "eat". The difference here is that our ancient cousins didn't believe that Adonai literally ate and drank.

GOLDEN MENORAH

25:31-40

You shall also make a *Menorah* of pure beaten gold. Its base, shaft, cups, *calyxes* and petals will all be cast from a single piece of gold.

Six stems will extend from the shaft: three on one side and three on the other. Each of the six branches will feature three cups shaped like almond blossoms, including calyxes and petals. On the main shaft there will be four almond blossom cups with calyxes and petals, (including one cup just below each point at which a pair of stems branches off from the main shaft). Mount the lamps so that they shine light from the front side.

Menorah: Literally, a "lamp stand" or "chandelier". The מְנֹרָה described here isn't any ordinary candelabra. It's THE מְנֹרָה, the seven-branched lamp built by Benay Yisra'el in the wilderness which became an important ritual object in the Beit Ha-Mikdash (Temple) in Yerushalayim (yes, that's the same Bayt Ha-Mikdash from our Haftarah). Don't confuse it with the nine-branched Ḥanukah menorah which is used to count off the days of Ḥanukah and which was never a holy object in the Beit Ha-Mikdash. The Menorah survived for over 1200 years until the Roman armies destroyed the Second Beit Ha-Mikdash in the year 70, looted the sacred objects, and carried them off to Rome. A carving showing the Roman troops carrying the Menorah and other objects can still be seen today on the Arch of Titus in Rome.

Calyxes: A calyx is the leafy, bulbous part of the flower that the petals grow out of.

Talent: This was the highest unit of weight used in the Tanaḥ (Jewish Bible). One talent equalled 3000 shekels. Today, the shekel is the official currency of the State of Israel, but in Ye Olden Dayes is was a unit of measurement, roughly 9.5 to 10.5 grams or one-third of an ounce (think of it as the Jewish equivalent to the British pound). So how much gold went into making the Menorah and its utensils? A lot. ☺

The mountain: Mount Sinai.

All of this must be hammered from a single piece of gold. The tongs and snuffers will be pure gold, as well. In all, the Menorah and its utensils shall be made from a single **talent** of pure gold. Mark this well and make sure you follow the design that is being shown to you on **the mountain!**

Warning: Read this first!

You're about to read a detailed description of what the Mishkan looked like. God's Message to Moshe included images as well as verbal instructions. When we read it, we don't have the benefit of a picture, so we have to use our imaginations. The Mishkan had three sections: (1) a large courtyard enclosed by hangings that were hung between wooden posts; (2) the Mikdash, which was a rectangular, box-shaped pavilion supported by a framework of vertical posts and horizontal poles. Huge tapestries were draped over the frame to give it solid walls. All this was covered by enormous canvases; (3) the Kodesh Ha-Kodashim, which was a chamber inside the Mikdash where God's Presence "lived".

If all this makes you think of a giant tent, you're right! Remember that at the time of the Torah, Benay Yisra'el lived in the Sinai wilderness. God's "House" not only had to fit in with its surroundings, it also had to be portable so that the Kohanim could easily dismantle it, move it, and set it back up again.

The following descriptions are divided into sections: (1) the wall tapestries that covered the frame; (2) the tent and the outer canvas that covered the whole Mishkan; (3) the wood frame; (4) the curtain that separated the Kodesh Ha-Kodashim from the outer part of the Mishkan; (5) the curtain that formed the entrance to the Mishkan.

Just how big was the Mishkan? Read through the chapter and see if you can figure it out (remember that an amah is roughly 18 inches / 0.5 meters). You may be surprised by what you find. To help with visualizing some of this, check out the Handy Floor Plan after the Haftarah in this guide.

MISHKAN MAKING

26: 1-6

PART ONE: WALL TAPESTRIES
FOR THE MIKDASH

Cover the frame of the Mishkan with ten tapestries woven from the highest quality blue, purple and crimson fabrics. Weave the image of a keruv into every one. Each tapestry will be twenty-eight amot long and four amot wide. Divide them into two sets of five and stitch them together

The Torah is describing a four-step process for making the enormous cover for the Mishkan's wood framework:

(1) Make ten tapestries, each one measuring 28 x 4 amot.

(2) Sew five of the tapestries together along their long sides to make a gigantic drapery 28 x 20 amot in size. Repeat with the other five tapestries.

(3) Add fifty fabric loops to the outer edges of both draperies. When the draperies are arranged side-by-side, make sure the loops match up.

(4) Use gold clasps to attach the two 28 x 20 draperies.

Once the frame was ready, this enormous drapery would have been... well, *draped* over it to form a solid ceiling and walls. To get a sense of size, recall that an amah (cubit) was equal to eighteen inches or half a meter. It may be time to whip out that calculator.

into two large draperies. Add fabric loops to the outermost edges of the draperies (fifty loops per drapery). Make fifty golden clasps and use them to attach the draperies so that the Mishkan becomes a single unit.

26: 7-14

PART TWO: THE MIKDASH'S TENT AND OUTER CANVAS

Make a tent of goats' hair to cover the Mishkan. Make it in eleven strips of cloth, each strip measuring thirty amot long and four amot wide. Stitch five of the strips together for one

Once the Mishkan's frame is set up and after it's covered by the rich tapestries from Part One, everything is covered by three more layers:

(1) A cloth tent woven from goats' hair, made from eleven strips 30 x 4 amot each;

(2) A canvas made from ram hide;

(3) A second canvas made from tahash hide.

half of the canvas and then stitch the remaining six strips together to make the other half (fold back the sixth strip to form the entrance to the tent). Add fifty loops to each of the outer edges and use fifty copper clasps to attach them, thereby making a single canvas tent. The tent will overhang the Mishkan on three sides: half of a cloth strip along the back and an amah of cloth on each side.

Cover the tent with two hide canvases: one of rams' hide and one of tahash hide.

26: 15-25

PART THREE: THE MIKDASH'S WOOD FRAME

The Mishkan's frame will be made from posts of acacia wood ten amot long and one and a half amot wide. Fix two pegs to the bottom of each post. The north and south sides of the Mishkan will require twenty posts. The rear of the Mishkan, which is the western side, will require eight posts: six to frame the wall and one for each corner.

Make one silver socket for each peg (two sockets for each post). Thus, there will be forty sockets for the northern side, forty for the southern side, and sixteen for the western side. Arrange the sockets on the ground and stand the posts upright by sliding their pegs into the sockets.

> ## 26: 26-30

Use bars of acacia wood as crosspieces to secure the posts. Each of the Mishkan's sides will require five bars, with the middle bar fitting through the center of each post. Coat the posts with gold and attach gold rings to the posts for the bars to slide through. Erect the Mishkan according to the design that was revealed to you on the mountain.

> ## 26: 31-35

PART FOUR: THE CURTAIN FOR THE KODESH HA-KODASHIM

Make a parohet from the highest quality blue, purple and crimson fabrics with the image

Parohet: This was the curtain that hung across the entrance to the Kodesh Ha-Kodashim where the Aron was kept. Parohets are still used today in synagogues. Where in the synagogue would you find one? What is it used for? Your rabbi / teacher can help you to compare and contrast modern and ancient sanctuaries.

of keruvim woven into it. Hang it from four pillars of acacia wood coated with gold and affixed with golden hooks. The posts will stand upright on four silver sockets. Use clasps to hold back the curtain when you bring the Aron inside. This curtain will be the partition between the Kodesh Ha-Kodashim and the Mikdash. Place a cover over the Aron.

Outside the Kodesh Ha-Kodashim, place the ritual table against the northern wall and the menorah directly across from it along the southern wall.

> ## 26: 36-37

PART FIVE: THE CURTAIN FOR THE MIKDASH'S ENTRANCE

Make a screen for the entrance to the Mishkan from embroidered blue, purple and crimson fabrics. Hang it from golden hooks attached to five pillars of acacia wood. Coat the pillars with gold and stand them upright on five silver sockets.

ALTARED STATES

27:1-8

*Make a square **altar** from wooden boards five amot to a side and three amot high, with **horns** at the four corners. The horns and the altar must be built from a single piece and coated with copper. The pots for removing ashes, scrapers, hooks, pans, basins — all the utensils — will also be made from copper. **The altar will be hollow** and will rest on a floor of copper grating. Fashion copper rings for the outside corners of the grating. Make two copper-coated wooden poles to fit through the rings so that the altar can be carried.*

Make everything according to the design you were shown on the mountain.

Altar: An altar is a special table that's used for burning sacrifices. In Ye Olden Dayes, most ancient cultures sacrificed to gods on altars.

Horns: It seems weird, but altars in ancient Israel were in fact designed with horns on the corners. Not actual animal horns, but horn shapes that were carved out of the altar itself. No-one knows exactly what the purpose of the horns was, but Psalm 118 mentions tying down festival offerings to the horns.

The altar will be hollow: Most altars had a flat tops just like a regular table. Here, the Torah describes something more like an open box, where the four sides rise up from the bottom to a height of three amot. Whatever was being sacrificed would be lowered down to the bottom and burned up. Since the bottom was a metal grate, the ashes simply fell through to the ground for cleanup later on.

ENCLOSURE

27:9-16

As for the Mishkan's courtyard, the southern side will be one hundred amot long. Space twenty posts evenly along it, stand them upright in twenty copper sockets, and connect them with silver rods. Fix silver hooks to the rods. Weave fine linen sheets and hang them from the hooks to cover the spaces between the posts. Do the same for the northern side. The western side will be fifty amot long and will include ten posts and ten sockets, along with the necessary hangings, rods and hooks.

The front of the courtyard, which is the eastern side, will be fifty amot long. For each side, make three posts with sockets and fifteen amot of hangings. The entrance will be twenty amot wide. Cover it with a fine linen curtain embroidered with blue, purple and crimson threads. Support it with four posts and sockets.

> **27: 17-19**
>
> This is the Maftir reading.

All the courtyard's posts will be embellished with silver bands. The hooks will be silver and the sockets will be copper. The enclosure will be one hundred amot long, fifty amot wide, and five amot high, with fine linen hangings suspended between the posts. The sockets for the posts, the utensils for the Mishkan's rituals, and all the pegs will be copper.

The utensils...: Earlier in the Parashah, didn't the Torah go through a lot of trouble to describe golden utensils for the Mishkan? It certainly did. The Mishkan featured two locations for religious observance. Public rituals took place in the courtyard outside the Mikdash on the big altar with the metal grate at the bottom. Separate from that, rituals meant only for Kohanim and VIP's took place in God's direct Presence inside the Mikdash (only the Kohen Ha-Gadol entered the Kodesh Ha-Kodashim). Utensils for these more private rituals were made of gold; utensils for the public rituals were made of copper. Which is fancier — gold or copper? Why distinguish between rituals for the public and rituals for the Kohanim? Your rabbi / teacher can help you explore this.

Think of what synagogues look like today. Is there a difference between the look and feel of the foyer versus the look and feel of the sanctuary? Think of a synagogue as a modern-day Mishkan. Are today's sanctuaries meant to imitate the feel of the Mikdash or its courtyard? Which part of the synagogue is meant to imitate the feel of the Kodesh Ha-Kodashim? How does all this help you understand why copper was used in the Mikdash's courtyard while gold was used in the Mikdash? Discuss your thoughts!

Reread the list of mandatory gifts at the beginning of the Parashah. Now that you know what everything was used for, why do you think it was necessary to give such expensive items? How does this help you understand the idea of the תְּרוּמָה — a mandatory gift? Can you think of anything we do today that compares to this? Your rabbi / teacher can help you explore your ideas.

Up next...

Tetzaveh! In *Terumah*, Benay Yisra'el received instructions for constructing the Mishkan and its tools. Next week, they receive directions on designing proper outfits for the Kohanim and officially assigning them to their jobs.

WEEKLY HAFTARAH

1 MELAHIM / KINGS 5: 26 TO 6: 13 IN ENGLISH

What's the story so far?

The time of the Torah has long since passed. After a long exile in Mitzra'im (Egypt), the nation of Yisra'el returns to Cana'an and establishes a kingdom under the leadership of David and Shlomo (Solomon) roughly 3000-ish years ago. Following Shlomo's death, a civil war breaks out that divides the kingdom into Yisra'el in the north and Yehudah in the south. The kingdoms coexist for 200 years until Yisra'el is conquered by Ashur (the Assyrian empire) in 722-720 BCE. Its leaders and many of its people are deported, and the kingdom is lost to history. Yehudah survives until Bavel (the Babylonian empire) conquers them, destroys Yerushalayim and the Bayt Ha-Mikdash (Temple to God), and exiles much of the population in 596-586 BCE. The two books of *Melahim* provide a history of these kingdoms from the time of King Shlomo to the destruction of Yehudah.

Who's Shlomo and why's he in our Haftarah?

Shlomo was the third king of ancient Yisra'el. The first king, Sha'ul, was unable to unite the various (and often feuding) tribes of Yisra'el, and he died in battle against the Pelishtim (Philistines). His famous general, David, was appointed king after him. David was wildly successful, uniting the tribes and expanding the borders of the kingdom to include most of the neighboring peoples. David's greatest accomplishments were the establishment of Yerushalayim (Jerusalem) as the eternal capital of the nation of Yisra'el (3000-ish years ago) and the establishment of his dynasty as the ruling family. His son, Shlomo, added to this success by building the first Bayt Ha-Mikdash, which remained the center of Yisra'el's worship until its destruction by Bavel more than 400 years later. Shlomo was also famous for his exceptional wisdom.

Our Haftarah describes the construction of the Bayt Ha-Mikdash. As you read through it, compare and contrast the description of the building of the Mishkan in our Parashah with the building of the Bayt Ha-Mikdash 250-ish years later. How are they similar? How are they different? How does the layout of the Bayt Ha-Mikdash compare to the layouts of synagogues today? Points to ponder.

And so, without further ado, on to the Haftarah...

MANDATORY "GIFTS"

| 5: 26-32 |

Fulfilling a commitment to Shlomo, Adonai granted the king wisdom. Shlomo and **Hiram** struck a treaty and there was peace between them.

Shlomo then **conscripted** a labor force from Yisra'el and placed it under Adoniram's supervision. They worked on rotations, with each worker spending one month in Lebanon and two months at home. Ten thousand workers were sent to Lebanon each month as lumberjacks while 20,000 worked in Yisra'el for a total of 30,000 conscripts per month. In all, Shlomo had 70,000 people moving raw materials and 80,000 people mining stone in the mountains. Shlomo assigned 3,300 officers to oversee all this work.

By the king's command, the people quarried massive, high quality stones so that the foundation of God's House could be made from cut stonework. Masons from Shlomo, Hiram, and the **Givlim** cut the stone and the lumber to build the House.

Hiram: Hiram was the king of Tyre, which was a Phoenician city-state on the coast of modern-day Lebanon. Tyre was famous for its shipbuilding, lumber, and construction industries.

Conscripted: This word is used when a government forces civilians into military or public service. People who are conscripted have no choice; they either report for duty or they go to prison. In Ye Olden Dayes, conscription was sometimes used by kings as a form of taxation. The conscription described in our Haftarah was a major factor that led to the civil war which split Shlomo's kingdom after his death.

Givlim: Who are these people? They're only mentioned in passing three times in the Tanah (Jewish Bible). Look for them in chapter 13 of *Yehoshu'a / Joshua*, chapter 27 of *Yehezk'el / Ezekiel*, and chapter 83 of *Tehilim / Psalms*. Geval is the Hebrew name for the ancient city of Byblos, which was located north of modern-day Beirut on the Lebanese coast.

The Parashah opens with God demanding a terumah (mandatory gift) from each person in Benay Yisra'el. How does the terumah compare to the mandatory "giving" that Shlomo demands here? Explore your ideas.

Mitzra'im: a.k.a. Egypt.

Ziv: In the time of the first Bayt Ha-Mikdash, our ancient cousins had different names for the months of the year than we use now. Their calendar started with Spring (that was the actual name), which was the month of Pesah. Ziv was the second month, which corresponds today to... what? Your rabbi / teacher can help you figure it out.

Amot: The אַמָּה (plural, אַמּוֹת) was an ancient unit of measurement. It's usually translated as "cubit". It was the distance from elbow to fingertip, roughly eighteen inches or half a meter. So how big was God's House in modern terms? I'll let you figure it out.

To help visualize the layout of the Bayt Ha-Mikdash and the Mishkan, check out the Handy Floor Plans after the Haftarah.

CONSTRUCTION PROJECT

| 6: 1-6 |

Shlomo started building Adonai's House in the four hundred and eightieth year after Benay Yisra'el's departure from **Mitzra'im**. It was the second month of his fourth year as king, the month of **Ziv**. Adonai's House was sixty **amot** long, twenty amot wide, and thirty amot high. The entryway which led into the House's main hall was ten amot long and twenty amot wide, and Shlomo installed narrow, beveled windows in the main hall.

Shlomo enclosed the House on three sides with a three-story structure that contained side chambers. The first story was five amot wide, the second story was six amot wide, and the top story was seven amot wide. To prevent the ceiling beams of the side chambers from penetrating the walls of the House, Shlomo made the outer walls of the House very thick, and he had grooves carved into the walls' exterior for the beams to fit into.

6:7-13

The stones used to build the House were cut and finished at the quarry. As a result, the sounds of hammers, axes, and iron tools were nowhere to be heard during the construction. The doorway to the first floor of the side-chambers was located to the right of the House, with winding stairs leading up to the second and third floors. Each floor of the side-chambers was five amot high, and they were secured to the House with cedar beams. Shlomo also added cedar beams and paneling to the House's ceiling after the structure was built.

Then a Message from Adonai came to Shlomo.

Regarding this House you are building for Me:

If you walk in My ways —
If you follow My Rules —
If you observe My Mitzvot and live by them —

I will fulfill the commitment with you that I made with your father, David:

I will live among Benay Yisra'el.
I will not leave My people, Yisra'el.

Our Haftarah only describes the Bayt Ha-Mikdash's basic structure. The next chapter and a half of Melakim go on to describe in great detail the stunning decorations, intricate finishings, and fantastic wealth that Shlomo put into it after the structure was built. To fully compare the Bayt Ha-Mikdash and the Mishkan, you should read these chapters.

Think about the two massive construction projects we see in the Parashah and the Haftarah. How are the Bayt Ha-Mikdash and the Mishkan alike? How are they different? How do modern synagogues resemble or differ from the Bayt Ha-Mikdash and the Mishkan? Your rabbi / teacher can help you explore your ideas!

HANDY FLOOR PLAN OF THE MISHKAN

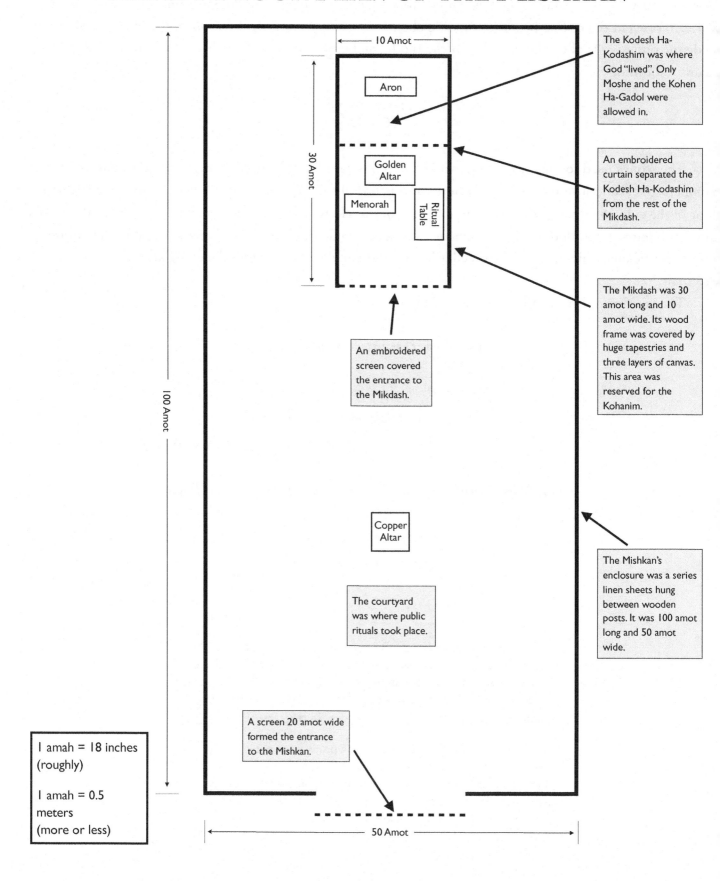

10 Amot

Aron

30 Amot

Golden Altar

Menorah

Ritual Table

The Kodesh Ha-Kodashim was where God "lived". Only Moshe and the Kohen Ha-Gadol were allowed in.

An embroidered curtain separated the Kodesh Ha-Kodashim from the rest of the Mikdash.

An embroidered screen covered the entrance to the Mikdash.

The Mikdash was 30 amot long and 10 amot wide. Its wood frame was covered by huge tapestries and three layers of canvas. This area was reserved for the Kohanim.

100 Amot

Copper Altar

The courtyard was where public rituals took place.

The Mishkan's enclosure was a series linen sheets hung between wooden posts. It was 100 amot long and 50 amot wide.

A screen 20 amot wide formed the entrance to the Mishkan.

1 amah = 18 inches (roughly)

1 amah = 0.5 meters (more or less)

50 Amot

HANDY FLOOR PLAN OF THE BAYT HA-MIKDASH

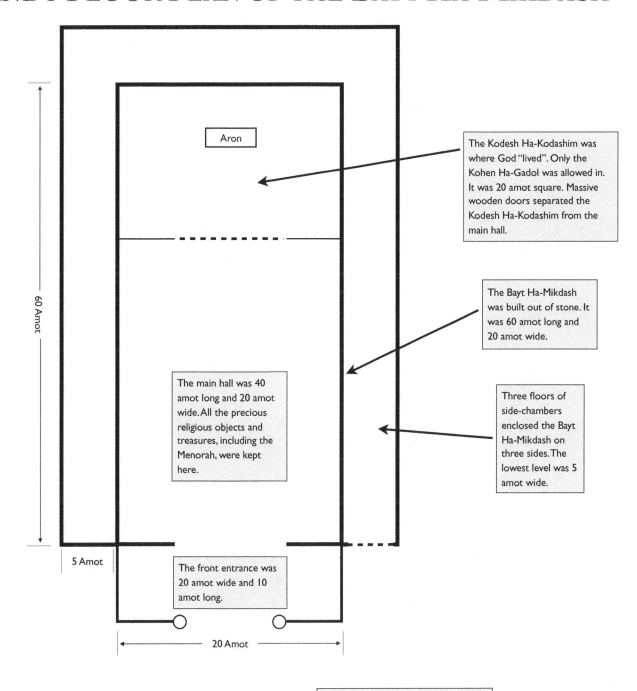

Aron

60 Amot

The Kodesh Ha-Kodashim was where God "lived". Only the Kohen Ha-Gadol was allowed in. It was 20 amot square. Massive wooden doors separated the Kodesh Ha-Kodashim from the main hall.

The Bayt Ha-Mikdash was built out of stone. It was 60 amot long and 20 amot wide.

The main hall was 40 amot long and 20 amot wide. All the precious religious objects and treasures, including the Menorah, were kept here.

Three floors of side-chambers enclosed the Bayt Ha-Mikdash on three sides. The lowest level was 5 amot wide.

5 Amot

The front entrance was 20 amot wide and 10 amot long.

20 Amot

Public sacrifices took place outside the Bayt Ha-Mikdash.

1 amah = 18 inches (roughly)

1 amah = 0.5 meters (more or less)

THE MAFTIR AND ITS BLESSINGS
(SHEMOT / EXODUS 27: 17-19)

Before the Torah reading, recite one of the following blessings.
Your rabbi or teacher will tell you which one is appropriate for your community.

You call out:	**You call out:**
בָּרְכוּ אֶת יְיָ הַמְבֹרָךְ.	בָּרְכוּ אֶת יְיָ הַמְבֹרָךְ.
The congregation responds:	**The congregation responds:**
בָּרוּךְ יְיָ הַמְבֹרָךְ לְעוֹלָם וָעֶד.	בָּרוּךְ יְיָ הַמְבֹרָךְ לְעוֹלָם וָעֶד.
You say it back to them:	**You say it back to them:**
בָּרוּךְ יְיָ הַמְבֹרָךְ לְעוֹלָם וָעֶד.	בָּרוּךְ יְיָ הַמְבֹרָךְ לְעוֹלָם וָעֶד.
You continue:	**You continue:**
בָּרוּךְ אַתָּה יְיָ אֱלֹהֵינוּ מֶלֶךְ הָעוֹלָם,	בָּרוּךְ אַתָּה יְיָ אֱלֹהֵינוּ מֶלֶךְ הָעוֹלָם,
אֲשֶׁר קֵרְבָנוּ לַעֲבוֹדָתוֹ	אֲשֶׁר בָּחַר בָּנוּ מִכָּל הָעַמִּים
וְנָתַן לָנוּ אֶת תּוֹרָתוֹ.	וְנָתַן לָנוּ אֶת תּוֹרָתוֹ.
בָּרוּךְ אַתָּה יְיָ, נוֹתֵן הַתּוֹרָה.	בָּרוּךְ אַתָּה יְיָ, נוֹתֵן הַתּוֹרָה.
Let us praise Adonai, the Blessed One!	Let us praise Adonai, the Blessed One!
Let Adonai, the Blessed One, be praised forever!	Let Adonai, the Blessed One, be praised forever!
We praise You, Adonai our God, Ruler of the universe, Who drew us close to God's Work and gave us God's Torah.	We praise You, Adonai our God, Ruler of the universe, Who chose us from all the nations to be given God's Torah.
We praise You, Adonai, the Giver of Torah.	We praise You, Adonai, the Giver of Torah.

עֶשְׂרִים אַמָּה תְּכֵלֶת וְאַרְגָּמָן וְתוֹלַעַת
שָׁנִי וְשֵׁשׁ מָשְׁזָר מַעֲשֵׂה רֹקֵם עַמֻּדֵיהֶם
אַרְבָּעָה וְאַדְנֵיהֶם אַרְבָּעָה כָּל עַמּוּדֵי
הֶחָצֵר סָבִיב מְחֻשָּׁקִים כֶּסֶף וָוֵיהֶם כֶּסֶף
וְאַדְנֵיהֶם נְחֹשֶׁת אֹרֶךְ הֶחָצֵר מֵאָה בָאַמָּה
וְרֹחַב חֲמִשִּׁים בַּחֲמִשִּׁים וְקֹמָה חָמֵשׁ
אַמּוֹת שֵׁשׁ מָשְׁזָר וְאַדְנֵיהֶם נְחֹשֶׁת לְכֹל
כְּלֵי הַמִּשְׁכָּן בְּכֹל עֲבֹדָתוֹ וְכָל יְתֵדֹתָיו
וְכָל יִתְדֹת הֶחָצֵר נְחֹשֶׁת וְאַתָּה תְּצַוֶּה
אֶת בְּנֵי יִשְׂרָאֵל וְיִקְחוּ אֵלֶיךָ שֶׁמֶן זַיִת
זָךְ כָּתִית לַמָּאוֹר לְהַעֲלֹת נֵר
תָּמִיד בְּאֹהֶל מוֹעֵד מִחוּץ לַפָּרֹכֶת אֲשֶׁר
עַל הָעֵדֻת יַעֲרֹךְ אֹתוֹ אַהֲרֹן וּבָנָיו מֵעֶרֶב
עַד בֹּקֶר לִפְנֵי יְהוָה חֻקַּת עוֹלָם לְדֹרֹתָם
מֵאֵת בְּנֵי יִשְׂרָאֵל וְאַתָּה הַקְרֵב
אֵלֶיךָ אֶת אַהֲרֹן אָחִיךָ וְאֶת בָּנָיו אִתּוֹ
מִתּוֹךְ בְּנֵי יִשְׂרָאֵל לְכַהֲנוֹ לִי אַהֲרֹן נָדָב
וַאֲבִיהוּא אֶלְעָזָר וְאִיתָמָר בְּנֵי אַהֲרֹן

19. לְכֹל כְּלֵי הַמִּשְׁכָּן

בְּכֹל עֲבֹדָתוֹ

וְכָל־יְתֵדֹתָיו

וְכָל־יִתְדֹת הֶחָצֵר נְחֹשֶׁת:

17. כָּל־עַמּוּדֵי הֶחָצֵר סָבִיב

מְחֻשָּׁקִים כֶּסֶף

וָוֵיהֶם כָּסֶף

וְאַדְנֵיהֶם נְחֹשֶׁת:

18. אֹרֶךְ הֶחָצֵר מֵאָה בָאַמָּה

וְרֹחַב | חֲמִשִּׁים בַּחֲמִשִּׁים

וְקֹמָה

חָמֵשׁ אַמּוֹת שֵׁשׁ מָשְׁזָר

וְאַדְנֵיהֶם נְחֹשֶׁת:

After the Torah reading, recite the following blessing.

בָּרוּךְ אַתָּה יְיָ אֱלֹהֵינוּ מֶלֶךְ הָעוֹלָם, אֲשֶׁר נָתַן לָנוּ תּוֹרַת אֱמֶת,

וְחַיֵּי עוֹלָם נָטַע בְּתוֹכֵנוּ. בָּרוּךְ אַתָּה יְיָ, נוֹתֵן הַתּוֹרָה.

We praise You, Adonai our God, Ruler of the universe,
Who planted eternal life among us by giving us a Teaching of truth.

We praise You, Adonai, the Giver of Torah.

THE HAFTARAH & ITS BLESSINGS
(1 MELAḤIM / KINGS 5: 26 TO 6: 13)

OPENING BLESSING

Before the Haftarah reading, recite one of the following blessings.
Your rabbi or teacher will tell you which one is appropriate for your community.

בָּרוּךְ אַתָּה יְיָ אֱלֹהֵינוּ מֶלֶךְ הָעוֹלָם,

אֲשֶׁר בָּחַר בִּנְבִיאִים טוֹבִים,

וְרָצָה בְדִבְרֵיהֶם הַנֶּאֱמָרִים בֶּאֱמֶת.

בָּרוּךְ אַתָּה יְיָ,

הַבּוֹחֵר בַּתּוֹרָה וּבְמֹשֶׁה עַבְדּוֹ,

וּבִנְבִיאֵי הָאֱמֶת וָצֶדֶק.

בָּרוּךְ אַתָּה יְיָ אֱלֹהֵינוּ מֶלֶךְ הָעוֹלָם,

אֲשֶׁר בָּחַר בִּנְבִיאִים טוֹבִים,

וְרָצָה בְדִבְרֵיהֶם הַנֶּאֱמָרִים בֶּאֱמֶת.

בָּרוּךְ אַתָּה יְיָ,

הַבּוֹחֵר בַּתּוֹרָה וּבְמֹשֶׁה עַבְדּוֹ,

וּבְיִשְׂרָאֵל עַמּוֹ,

וּבִנְבִיאֵי הָאֱמֶת וָצֶדֶק.

We praise You, Adonai our God,
Ruler of the universe,
Who appointed good prophets,
and Who expected lessons of truth
in the things they said.

We praise You, Adonai,
Who chose the Torah,
and Moshe, God's servant,
and prophets of truth and righteousness.

We praise You, Adonai our God,
Ruler of the universe,
Who appointed good prophets,
and Who expected lessons of truth
in the things they said.

We praise You, Adonai,
Who chose the Torah,
and Moshe, God's servant,
and Yisra'el, God's people,
and prophets of truth and righteousness.

Chapter 5

29. וַיְהִי לִשְׁלֹמֹה
שִׁבְעִים אֶלֶף נֹשֵׂא סַבָּל
וּשְׁמֹנִים אֶלֶף חֹצֵב בָּהָר:

30. לְבַד
מִשָּׂרֵי הַנִּצָּבִים לִשְׁלֹמֹה
אֲשֶׁר עַל־הַמְּלָאכָה
שְׁלֹשֶׁת אֲלָפִים וּשְׁלֹשׁ מֵאוֹת
הָרֹדִים בָּעָם
הָעֹשִׂים בַּמְּלָאכָה:

31. וַיְצַו הַמֶּלֶךְ
וַיַּסִּעוּ אֲבָנִים גְּדֹלוֹת
אֲבָנִים יְקָרוֹת
לְיַסֵּד הַבָּיִת אַבְנֵי גָזִית:

32. וַיִּפְסְלוּ
בֹּנֵי שְׁלֹמֹה
וּבֹנֵי חִירוֹם וְהַגִּבְלִים
וַיָּכִינוּ
הָעֵצִים וְהָאֲבָנִים לִבְנוֹת הַבָּיִת:

26. וַיהֹוָה
נָתַן חָכְמָה לִשְׁלֹמֹה
כַּאֲשֶׁר דִּבֶּר־לוֹ
וַיְהִי שָׁלֹם
בֵּין חִירָם וּבֵין שְׁלֹמֹה
וַיִּכְרְתוּ בְרִית שְׁנֵיהֶם:

27. וַיַּעַל הַמֶּלֶךְ שְׁלֹמֹה
מַס מִכָּל־יִשְׂרָאֵל
וַיְהִי הַמַּס
שְׁלֹשִׁים אֶלֶף אִישׁ:

28. וַיִּשְׁלָחֵם לְבָנוֹנָה
עֲשֶׂרֶת אֲלָפִים בַּחֹדֶשׁ חֲלִיפוֹת
חֹדֶשׁ יִהְיוּ בַלְּבָנוֹן
שְׁנַיִם חֳדָשִׁים בְּבֵיתוֹ
וַאֲדֹנִירָם עַל־הַמַּס:

8. פֶּתַח

הַצֵּלָע הַתִּיכֹנָה

אֶל־כֶּתֶף הַבַּיִת הַיְמָנִית

וּבְלוּלִּים

יַעֲלוּ עַל־הַתִּיכֹנָה

וּמִן־הַתִּיכֹנָה אֶל־הַשְּׁלִשִׁים:

9. וַיִּבֶן אֶת־הַבַּיִת וַיְכַלֵּהוּ

וַיִּסְפֹּן אֶת־הַבַּיִת גֵּבִים

וּשְׂדֵרֹת בָּאֲרָזִים:

10. וַיִּבֶן אֶת־הַיצוע [הַיָּצִיעַ]

עַל־כָּל־הַבַּיִת

חָמֵשׁ אַמּוֹת קוֹמָתוֹ

וַיֶּאֱחֹז אֶת־הַבַּיִת בַּעֲצֵי אֲרָזִים:

11. וַיְהִי דְּבַר־יְהוָה

אֶל־שְׁלֹמֹה לֵאמֹר:

6. הַיצוע [הַיָּצִיעַ] הַתַּחְתֹּנָה

חָמֵשׁ בָּאַמָּה רָחְבָּהּ

וְהַתִּיכֹנָה

שֵׁשׁ בָּאַמָּה רָחְבָּהּ

וְהַשְּׁלִישִׁית

שֶׁבַע בָּאַמָּה רָחְבָּהּ

כִּי

מִגְרָעוֹת נָתַן לַבַּיִת סָבִיב חוּצָה

לְבִלְתִּי אֲחֹז בְּקִירוֹת הַבָּיִת:

7. וְהַבַּיִת בְּהִבָּנֹתוֹ

אֶבֶן שְׁלֵמָה מַסָּע נִבְנָה

וּמַקָּבוֹת וְהַגַּרְזֶן כָּל־כְּלִי בַרְזֶל

לֹא־נִשְׁמַע בַּבַּיִת בְּהִבָּנֹתוֹ:

Chapter 6

.1 וַיְהִ֣י בִשְׁמוֹנִ֣ים שָׁנָ֗ה וְאַרְבַּ֣ע מֵא֣וֹת שָׁנָ֡ה לְצֵ֣את בְּנֵֽי־יִשְׂרָאֵ֣ל מֵאֶ֣רֶץ־מִצְרַ֩יִם֩ בַּשָּׁנָ֨ה הָרְבִיעִ֜ית בְּחֹ֣דֶשׁ זִ֗ו ה֚וּא הַחֹ֣דֶשׁ הַשֵּׁנִ֔י לִמְלֹ֥ךְ שְׁלֹמֹ֖ה עַל־יִשְׂרָאֵ֑ל וַיִּ֥בֶן הַבַּ֖יִת לַיהֹוָֽה׃

.2 וְהַבַּ֗יִת אֲשֶׁ֨ר בָּנָ֜ה הַמֶּ֤לֶךְ שְׁלֹמֹה֙ לַֽיהֹוָ֔ה שִׁשִּֽׁים־אַמָּ֤ה אׇרְכּוֹ֙ וְעֶשְׂרִ֣ים רׇחְבּ֔וֹ וּשְׁלֹשִׁ֥ים אַמָּ֖ה קֽוֹמָתֽוֹ׃

.3 וְהָֽאוּלָ֡ם עַל־פְּנֵי֩ הֵיכַ֨ל הַבַּ֜יִת עֶשְׂרִ֧ים אַמָּ֣ה אׇרְכּ֗וֹ עַל־פְּנֵ֖י רֹ֣חַב הַבָּ֑יִת עֶ֧שֶׂר בָּאַמָּ֛ה רׇחְבּ֖וֹ עַל־פְּנֵ֥י הַבָּֽיִת׃

.4 וַיַּ֣עַשׂ לַבָּ֑יִת חַלּוֹנֵ֖י שְׁקֻפִ֥ים אֲטֻמִֽים׃

.5 וַיִּ֩בֶן֩ עַל־קִ֨יר הַבַּ֤יִת יָצ֨וּעַ [יָצִ֨יעַ֙] סָבִ֔יב אֶת־קִיר֤וֹת הַבַּ֨יִת֙ סָבִ֔יב לַֽהֵיכָ֖ל וְלַדְּבִ֑יר וַיַּ֥עַשׂ צְלָע֖וֹת סָבִֽיב׃

13. וְשָׁכַנְתִּ֗י   12. הַבַּ֖יִת הַזֶּ֣ה אֲשֶׁר־אַתָּ֣ה בֹנֶ֑ה

בְּתֽוֹךְ בְּנֵ֣י יִשְׂרָאֵ֑ל   אִם־תֵּלֵ֣ךְ בְּחֻקֹּתַ֗י

וְלֹ֥א אֶעֱזֹ֖ב אֶת־עַמִּ֥י יִשְׂרָאֵֽל׃   וְאֶת־מִשְׁפָּטַ֤י תַּֽעֲשֶׂה֙

                                      וְשָׁמַרְתָּ֥ אֶת־כָּל־מִצְוֺתַ֖י

                                      לָלֶ֣כֶת בָּהֶ֑ם

                                      וַהֲקִמֹתִ֤י אֶת־דְּבָרִי֙ אִתָּ֔ךְ

                                      אֲשֶׁ֥ר דִּבַּ֖רְתִּי אֶל־דָּוִ֥ד אָבִֽיךָ׃

CLOSING BLESSINGS

After the Haftarah reading, four blessings are recited. Note that there are choices for some of them. Your rabbi or teacher will tell you which ones are appropriate for your community.

בָּרוּךְ אַתָּה יְיָ אֱלֹהֵינוּ מֶלֶךְ הָעוֹלָם, צוּר כָּל הָעוֹלָמִים, צַדִּיק בְּכָל הַדּוֹרוֹת,

הָאֵל הַנֶּאֱמָן הָאוֹמֵר וְעֹשֶׂה, הַמְדַבֵּר וּמְקַיֵּם, שֶׁכָּל דְּבָרָיו אֱמֶת וָצֶדֶק.

נֶאֱמָן אַתָּה הוּא יְיָ אֱלֹהֵינוּ, וְנֶאֱמָנִים דְּבָרֶיךָ,

וְדָבָר אֶחָד מִדְּבָרֶיךָ אָחוֹר לֹא יָשׁוּב רֵיקָם, כִּי אֵל מֶלֶךְ נֶאֱמָן וְרַחֲמָן אָתָּה.

בָּרוּךְ אַתָּה יְיָ, הָאֵל הַנֶּאֱמָן בְּכָל דְּבָרָיו.

We praise You, Adonai our God, Ruler of the universe, Creator of all the worlds,
righteous in every generation. The faithful God Who does what God says,
Who speaks and fulfills it, Whose every word is true and just.

Adonai our God, You are faithful, Your words are faithful,
and nothing You say ever goes unfulfilled. You are a faithful and merciful God and Ruler.
We praise You, Adonai, the God who is faithful in every word.

רַחֵם עַל צִיּוֹן כִּי הִיא בֵּית חַיֵּינוּ, וּלְעַמְּךָ יִשְׂרָאֵל תּוֹשִׁיעַ בִּמְהֵרָה בְיָמֵינוּ. בָּרוּךְ אַתָּה יְיָ, מְשַׂמֵּחַ צִיּוֹן בְּבָנֶיהָ.	רַחֵם עַל צִיּוֹן כִּי הִיא בֵּית חַיֵּינוּ, וְלַעֲלוּבַת נֶפֶשׁ תּוֹשִׁיעַ בִּמְהֵרָה בְיָמֵינוּ. בָּרוּךְ אַתָּה יְיָ, מְשַׂמֵּחַ צִיּוֹן בְּבָנֶיהָ.
Show compassion for Tzion, for she is our lifelong home. Redeem Your people Israel soon and in our lifetime.	Show compassion for Tzion, for she is our lifelong home. Redeem her distressed spirit soon and in our lifetime.
We praise You, Adonai, Who enables Tzion to rejoice with her children.	We praise you, Adonai, Who enables Tzion to rejoice with her children.

שַׂמְּחֵנוּ, יְיָ אֱלֹהֵינוּ,

בְּאֵלִיָּהוּ הַנָּבִיא עַבְדֶּךָ,

וּבְמַלְכוּת בֵּית דָּוִד מְשִׁיחֶךָ.

בִּמְהֵרָה יָבֹא וְיָגֵל לִבֵּנוּ,

עַל כִּסְאוֹ לֹא יֵשֶׁב זָר,

וְלֹא יִנְחֲלוּ עוֹד אֲחֵרִים אֶת כְּבוֹדוֹ,

כִּי בְשֵׁם קָדְשְׁךָ נִשְׁבַּעְתָּ לּוֹ

שֶׁלֹּא יִכְבֶּה נֵרוֹ לְעוֹלָם וָעֶד.

בָּרוּךְ אַתָּה יְיָ, מָגֵן דָּוִד.

Adonai our God,
grant us joy in Eliyahu Your prophet
and servant, and in the reign of the dynasty
of David, Your anointed king.
May he come soon and lift our hearts.
Let no stranger sit on his throne.
Let others no longer inherit his glory,
for You swore to him by Your holy Name
that his light would never go out.
We praise You, Adonai,
Shield of David.

שַׂמְּחֵנוּ, יְיָ אֱלֹהֵינוּ,

בְּאֵלִיָּהוּ הַנָּבִיא עַבְדֶּךָ,

בִּמְהֵרָה יָבֹא וְיָגֵל לִבֵּנוּ.

וְהֵשִׁיב לֵב אָבוֹת עַל בָּנִים

וְלֵב בָּנִים עַל אֲבוֹתָם,

וּבֵיתְךָ בֵּית תְּפִלָּה יִקָּרֵא לְכָל

הָעַמִּים.

בָּרוּךְ אַתָּה יְיָ, מֵבִיא שָׁלוֹם לָעַד.

Adonai our God,
grant us joy in Eliyahu Your prophet and
servant. Come soon to lift our hearts.
Turn the hearts of parents to their children,
and the hearts of children to their parents.
May Your House be called
a House of Prayer for all nations.
We praise You, Adonai,
Who brings peace for all time.

עַל הַתּוֹרָה, וְעַל הָעֲבוֹדָה, וְעַל הַנְּבִיאִים, וְעַל יוֹם הַשַּׁבָּת הַזֶּה,

שֶׁנָּתַתָּ לָּנוּ, יְיָ אֱלֹהֵינוּ, לִקְדֻשָּׁה וְלִמְנוּחָה, לְכָבוֹד וּלְתִפְאָרֶת.

עַל הַכֹּל, יְיָ אֱלֹהֵינוּ, אֲנַחְנוּ מוֹדִים לָךְ, וּמְבָרְכִים אוֹתָךְ,

יִתְבָּרַךְ שִׁמְךָ בְּפִי כָּל חַי תָּמִיד לְעוֹלָם וָעֶד.

בָּרוּךְ אַתָּה יְיָ, מְקַדֵּשׁ הַשַּׁבָּת.

For the Torah, for our worship, for the prophets, for today's Shabbat that
You, Adonai our God, gave us for holiness, rest, glory, and wonder:
for everything, Adonai our God, we thank You and praise You.
May the lips of every living thing glorify Your Name forever.

We praise You, Adonai, Who makes Shabbat holy.

SHABBAT ROSH HODESH READINGS

BA-MIDBAR / NUMBERS 28: 9-15

What's the story so far?

If you've read the blurbs for the Parashah or the Haftarah, you'll know that this is the spot that describes the events that lead up to the weekly Torah reading. But when it comes to Rosh Hodesh, there isn't really a "story so far" because the monthly celebration happens outside of the weekly reading cycle. The piece of Torah we read on Shabbat changes every week as we move through the year, but the pieces of Torah we read for Rosh Hodesh and the Hagim (annual festivals) stay the same. In other words, whenever Rosh Hodesh falls on a weekday, the Torah reading is always *Bamidbar / Numbers* 28: 1-15. The only exception is when Rosh Hodesh coincides with Shabbat. When that happens, we add *Bamidbar / Numbers* 28: 9-15 to the regular Shabbat reading, and we usually replace the regular Shabbat Haftarah with *Yish'ayah / Isaiah* 66: 1-24.

Rosh Hodesh means "head of the month". As you might guess, the Torah reading for Shabbat Rosh Hodesh is connected to the festival of the new moon when we mark the beginning of a new month. Check out the night sky. If the moon appears as a tiny sliver — or not at all — then you know it's Rosh Hodesh. Nowadays, marking the new month isn't a big deal, and many Jews haven't heard of Rosh Hodesh. But back in Ye Olden Dayes, when there were no such things as internet, TV, or printed calendars, declaring the new month was serious business. All the Hagim are connected to specific days of the month: Pesah begins on the 14th day of the first month, Yom Kippur begins on the 10th day of the seventh month, etc. Marking Rosh Hodesh was the key to ensuring that everything ran on time.

What can I expect from this Parashah?

The Torah reading for Shabbat Rosh Hodesh is an excerpt from Parashat *Pinhas*. It's preoccupied with sacrifices. These included meats, liquids and grains. It's easy to just dismiss it as ancient superstition or too much detail, butt before you do, consider for a moment the purpose behind it all. Why all the fuss? Why insist on such precision? What's the big deal? Your rabbi / teacher can help you with this.

And so, without further ado, on to the Torah!

Warning: Read this first!

You'll notice that all the offerings described here follow the same pattern: meat, dough (i.e. bread), and a drink (the meat and dough were burnt up on the altar, and the drink was poured over the altar). Meat, dough, drink. Why would a God that has no physical form demand a full meal as a form of worship? Meat, bread, drink. Does this sound familiar? How did our ancient cousins show respect for kings, queens, and honored guests? Look into the stories of Avraham and see what you come up with. Your rabbi / teacher can help you.

ATTENTION TO DETAIL

28: 9-15

The Message from God to Moshe continued:

On Shabbat, you will offer two year-old lambs that have no flaws or imperfections. Along with the lambs, you will include two-tenths of an efah of flour mixed with oil, and you will add the drink offering. These are in addition to the regular daily offerings.

There will be a fiery offering for the Rosh Hodesh festival, as well: two young bulls, one ram, and seven year-old lambs without any flaws or imperfections. With each bull, you will include three-tenths of an efah of flour and oil. With the ram, you will include two-tenths of an efah of flour and oil. With each lamb, you will include one-tenth of an efah of flour and oil. The drink offerings will be wine: one-half of a hin for each bull, one-third of a hin for the ram, and one-quarter of a hin for each lamb. This is the monthly offering for the Rosh Hodesh. It will be a pleasant aroma for Adonai.

No flaws or imperfections: Consider a farmer who has a sickly ox he can't use. He has to get rid of it, so he figures that if he offers it to God, he doesn't have to give up any of his good, productive oxen. Not much of a sacrifice, is it? Offerings to God had to come from the best of what a person owned. The donor had to feel as if s/he was giving up something truly important as a way of showing devotion to God.

Efah & hin: these were ancient units of measurement. An *efah* was around 36 liters or quarts. A *hin* was roughly 6 liters or quarts. So how much flour and oil are we talking about here? I'll let you do the math.

If you're used to a Conservative or Orthodox prayer tradition, this first paragraph should sound familiar (it might help to see it in Hebrew. You'll find it in the Hebrew section of this book). Where else do you encounter it? Hint: think of the extra Musaf service on Shabbat, Rosh Hodesh, and Hagim.

How did they remember all these details, and why do we have to (re)read them every month? In Ye Olden Dayes, the only people who really needed to know this stuff were the Kohanim (priests). Think of this as a kind of priestly textbook — a manual to teach ritual leaders everything they need to know about the proper ways to approach God in the right sequence. Hmm... this sounds familiar. Is there anything we use today that might fit this description?

Hatat: In general, there were six kinds of fiery offerings made to God in ancient times. Up to now, the Torah's been talking about an עֹלָה, which was the most common type of offering. It was used every day, on Shabbat, and on the festivals as a way of approaching God and expressing one's acceptance of the divine commandments. A חַטָאת offering was different. The goal here was to make amends for breaking any of the commandments unintentionally.

Why do you think it was necessary to make a חַטָאת offering on top of the other offerings that were already being made for Rosh Hodesh? What's the lesson here as we begin a new month?

In addition to the regular fire and drink offerings, you will offer a single male goat as a Hatat to Adonai.

SHABBAT ROSH HODESH HAFTARAH

YISH'AYAH / ISAIAH 66: 1-24

What's the story so far?

The time of the Torah has long since passed. After a long exile in Mitzra'im (Egypt), the nation of Yisra'el returns to Cana'an (the ancient name for Yisra'el) and establishes a kingdom under the leadership of David and Shlomo (roughly 3000-ish years ago). Following Shlomo's death, a civil war divides the kingdom into Yisra'el in the north and Yehudah in the south. The kingdoms coexist for 200 years until Yisra'el is conquered by Ashur (the Assyrian empire) in 722-720 BCE. Its people are deported and lost to history. Yehudah survives until Bavel (the Babylonians) conquers it and exiles the population in 597-586 BCE.

Who's Yish'ayah and why does he have a book?

Yish'ayah was a prophet of God. A "prophet" refers to someone who has a special gift for communicating God's inspiring message to the people, leaders, and — quite often — kings of Yisra'el. Some prophets were employees of the king. Others were recognized as community leaders. Still others travelled from place to place spreading word of God's ethical requirements. Some are recorded as having performed miracles. The time of the prophets stretches from Moshe (3200-ish years ago) to Mal'ahi (2400-ish years ago). Regardless of who they were or when they lived, they all felt the same divine calling to leave their professions and become God's social and moral conscience to the people.

The book of *Yish'ayah* is actually a compilation of at least two different prophets who lived roughly 200 years apart. Chapters one to thirty-nine belong to the first Yish'ayah who lived 2800-ish years ago during the time of the kings of Yisra'el. Chapters forty to sixty-six belong to the second Yish'ayah who lived some time during the Babylonian Exile, 2600-ish years ago.

What can I expect from this Haftarah?

The Haftarah for Shabbat Rosh Hodesh comes from the second Yish'ayah who lived during the Exile in Bavel (Babylon). He was very interested in trying to justify the destruction of the Jewish kingdoms, of Yerushalayim, and of the Bayt Ha-Mikdash (Temple to God). How could God allow these things to happen? How can Jewish culture survive without a homeland? What will the future hold for the Jewish people? What changes need to be made to Jewish culture to enable it to survive? Is there hope of a return to the land promised to our ancestors? These were his main concerns. As you read through the Haftarah, see if you can figure out why the early rabbis chose to connect this section of *Yish'ayah* to Rosh Hodesh.

And so, without further ado, on to the Haftarah...

Warning: Read this first!

Yish'ayah wasn't a journalist or a blogger. He was a public speaker. His book is a record of some of the speeches he gave in markets and other public spaces. He uses creative metaphors to make his points, and he alternates between speaking in his own voice and supplying dialogue for God. If you close your eyes, you can even imagine some of his listeners heckling him. Some of the most vivid (and sometimes disturbing) imagery in the entire Tanah (Jewish Bible) comes from Yish'ayah, and his messages are often very difficult to understand. Your rabbi / teacher can help you.

REASON FOR THE EXILE

66: 1-2

This is Adonai's Message:

The heavens are My throne, the earth My footrest. What sort of House could you build for Me? What sort of place could serve Me as a home?

Remember that Yish'ayah's audience was the Jewish exiles in Babylon who yearned to return to Yisra'el to rebuild Yerushalayim and the Bayt Ha-Mikdash (God's holy Temple). How is the message here a response to that yearning? What's Yish'ayah saying to these people about God's need to have a physical home?

Everything was made by My Hand — this was how everything came to be.

This is Adonai's vision!

These are the people I focus on: the poor, the downtrodden, and those who show genuine concern for My Words.

66: 3-4

As for people who slaughter oxen but slay humans...

As for people who sacrifice lambs but crack dogs' necks...

As for people who offer their Minhah with pig's blood...

As for people who burn sacred incense to bless idols...

They have made their choices! Their souls rejoice in these abominations!

I will also make a choice. I will mock them. I will make their fears reality. When I called they ignored. When I spoke they did not hear. They committed actions that are evil in My eyes and made choices I did not approve of.

Minhah: The מִנְחָה (Minhah) was an offering of flour and oil that accompanied most of the meat sacrifices.

Adonai is complaining about people who go through the motions of worship God properly (sacrificing oxen, lambs, the Minhah food offering, and burning incense) but also commit horrible acts (killing people and dogs, offering pig's blood, blessing idols).

Think about Yish'ayah's audience. They probably asked all sorts of questions about why Adonai let the kingdom of Yehudah fall and why the exile feels endless. What do you think of Yish'ayah's answer? Explore your ideas.

66: 5-6

You say you're concerned about Adonai's Words? Hear God's Words now!

Your fellow Yisra'elites who hate you and reject you because of Me say to you, "Go and glorify Adonai! Let us see the One Who gives you joy!" Yet they are the ones who will be shamed. Do you hear the thundering tumult from the city that comes from the Sanctuary? That is the thunder of Adonai repaying God's enemies!

Yish'ayah is responding to divisions within the Yisra'elite community. Some remained faithful to God's Mitzvot throughout the Exile while others rejected them out of anger. Here, God is mocking the people who refused to maintain their faith.

COMFORT AND HOPE

66: 7-11

Can a pregnant woman deliver a child before entering labor? Can she give birth before her pain comes? Who ever heard of such a thing? Who ever saw such a thing? Can land spring forth in a day? Is a nation born all at once? Yet **Tzion** labored and gave birth all at once!

Tzion: a.k.a. Yerushalayim.

This section is hard to understand. Yish'ayah is comparing Yerushalayim to a mother who gives birth to a baby without labor pains and then breastfeeds it. It's a miraculous birth — no pain or discomfort — because the baby literally just pops out. If the mother represents Yerushalayim, who or what does her baby represent? What's the message about the relationship between Yerushalayim and the people of Yisra'el?

When a mother coddles her baby at her breast, is the baby comforted or agitated? When a baby breastfeeds, does the baby feel threatened or safe? How does this help you understand what Yish'ayah is saying here about newborn babies and the exiles of Yisra'el?

Should I, Who causes labor, not cause birth—

—asks Adonai?

Should I, Who causes birth, close the womb—

—asks your God?

Rejoice with Yerushalayim! Let all who love her be glad! Let all who mourn her rejoice! Like a newborn sucking at its mother's breast, draw comfort from Yerushalayim's glory and be nourished.

66: 12-16

Hear Adonai's Message:

I will bring the calm of a flowing river to Yerushalayim. I will bring the glory of nations like a flooding stream! You will drink from it and be coddled by

Some people find the violence in this section hard to read. Is God really going to come down in a flaming whirlwind to cut down our enemies with a sword? Remember that Yish'ayah like to use metaphors. Focus less on the literal meaning of the text and more on the poetry. What is Yish'ayah saying about the future of Yisra'el and its culture?

Remember that Yish'ayah's audience had recently experienced the horrible violence and burning destruction of the Exile. In its own way, it was as traumatic for our ancient cousins as the Holocaust was in the last century. How might the Jewish exiles have felt when they heard Yish'ayah's words? Discuss your ideas!

it. I will comfort you the way a mother comforts her child, and you will find solace in Yerushalayim. When you see this your heart will rejoice and you will grow tall like grass.

When Adonai's Power defeats God's enemies, then Adonai's Power will be obvious to God's servants! Don't you see? Adonai is coming in a raging fire — coming on chariots in a whirlwind of flame — to bring divine fury and a fiery rebuke. Adonai will judge by fire, the verdict will be handed down by sword. The number slain by Adonai will be many.

66: 17-21

As for those who purify themselves to enter sacred groves —
As for those who eat pig, mice, and disgusting things —

I know their acts and their thoughts. They shall all meet their end!

This is Adonai's Vision!

A time is coming when all nations will gather to witness My Glory. I will send out survivors to spread word of My Glory to all the nations who do not know of Me — to the archers of Tarshish, Pul, and Lud; to Tuval, Yavan, and the distant isles. They shall bring your fellow Yisra'elites out of exile on horses, chariots, litters, mules, and camels, and deliver them to My holy mountain,

They shall bring out your fellow Yisra'elites...: Only the wealthiest people could afford to travel by horse, chariot, litter, and such. Benay Yisra'el entered Exile as a defeated, impoverished people. According to Yish'ayah, how will they leave the Exile? Does this idea remind you of another "exile" where God rescued Benay Yisra'el? Hint: check out the first half of the book of *Shemot / Exodus*. When they were finally let go, did they leave as a defeated people or a triumphant people? Compare and contrast the these two exiles and rescues.

Kohanim... Levi'im: כֹּהֵן means "priest". In Ye Olden Dayes, there was no such thing as a rabbi or a cantor. Instead, religious leaders came from the tribe of Levi. There were two types: כֹּהֲנִים who led the main sacrificial rituals and לְוִיִּם who led the choirs, the musical accompaniment, and who assisted the כֹּהֲנִים. Today, Judaism isn't led by priests, though the descendants of the ancient Kohanim and Levi'im are given special honors in many congregations (the Kohanim in some synagogues bless the congregation using the same blessing our ancient cousins used). Christianity has priests, but their jobs are different from the ancient כֹּהֲנִים. To avoid confusion between modern and ancient "priests", I've decided to use the Hebrew terms instead of the English.

Yerushalayim. When they arrive, Benay Yisra'el will bring their Minhah to the House of Adonai in a purified container, and I will appoint Kohanim and Levi'im from among them.

66: 22-24

I will make new heavens and new earth. Just as they will survive, so shall your descendants and your name survive.

This is Adonai's Vision.

Then month after month, and Shabbat after Shabbat, every living thing shall worship Me.

—says Adonai.

They shall go out and gaze at the bodies of those who rebelled against Me. The worms that crawl through the bodies will never die, nor will the flaming remains ever go out. These bodies will be treated with disgust by all living things.

Then month after month, and Shabbat after Shabbat, every living thing shall worship Me.

—says Adonai.

No, you aren't seeing a typo. Yish'ayah's book ends with the ominous image we see here of the bodies of God's enemies being disfigured for all eternity by fire and worms and being treated with disgust by all living things. While this gives the book a very dramatic ending, it's a bit depressing when read as a Haftarah. To end the Haftarah on a more positive note, our great sages decided to repeat verse 23, and they wrote it in smaller print so that people would see the difference between the ending of the Haftarah and the actual ending of *Yish'ayah*.

THE MAFTIR AND ITS BLESSINGS
(BA-MIDBAR / NUMBERS 28: 9-15)

Before the Torah reading, recite one of the following blessings.
Your rabbi or teacher will tell you which one is appropriate for your community.

You call out:	**You call out:**
בָּרְכוּ אֶת יְיָ הַמְבֹרָךְ.	בָּרְכוּ אֶת יְיָ הַמְבֹרָךְ.
The congregation responds:	**The congregation responds:**
בָּרוּךְ יְיָ הַמְבֹרָךְ לְעוֹלָם וָעֶד.	בָּרוּךְ יְיָ הַמְבֹרָךְ לְעוֹלָם וָעֶד.
You say it back to them:	**You say it back to them:**
בָּרוּךְ יְיָ הַמְבֹרָךְ לְעוֹלָם וָעֶד.	בָּרוּךְ יְיָ הַמְבֹרָךְ לְעוֹלָם וָעֶד.
You continue:	**You continue:**
בָּרוּךְ אַתָּה יְיָ אֱלֹהֵינוּ מֶלֶךְ הָעוֹלָם,	בָּרוּךְ אַתָּה יְיָ אֱלֹהֵינוּ מֶלֶךְ הָעוֹלָם,
אֲשֶׁר קֵרְבָנוּ לַעֲבוֹדָתוֹ	אֲשֶׁר בָּחַר בָּנוּ מִכָּל הָעַמִּים
וְנָתַן לָנוּ אֶת תּוֹרָתוֹ.	וְנָתַן לָנוּ אֶת תּוֹרָתוֹ.
בָּרוּךְ אַתָּה יְיָ, נוֹתֵן הַתּוֹרָה.	בָּרוּךְ אַתָּה יְיָ, נוֹתֵן הַתּוֹרָה.
Let us praise Adonai, the Blessed One!	Let us praise Adonai, the Blessed One!
Let Adonai, the Blessed One, be praised forever!	Let Adonai, the Blessed One, be praised forever!
We praise You, Adonai our God, Ruler of the universe, Who drew us close to God's Work and gave us God's Torah.	We praise You, Adonai our God, Ruler of the universe, Who chose us from all the nations to be given God's Torah.
We praise You, Adonai, the Giver of Torah.	We praise You, Adonai, the Giver of Torah.

14. וְנִסְכֵּיהֶם

חֲצִי הַהִין יִהְיֶה לַפָּר

וּשְׁלִישִׁת הַהִין לָאַיִל

וּרְבִיעִת הַהִין

לַכֶּבֶשׂ יָיִן

זֹאת עֹלַת חֹדֶשׁ בְּחָדְשׁוֹ

לְחָדְשֵׁי הַשָּׁנָה:

15. וּשְׂעִיר עִזִּים אֶחָד

לְחַטָּאת לַיהוָה

עַל־עֹלַת הַתָּמִיד

יֵעָשֶׂה וְנִסְכּוֹ:

בהר סיני לריח ניחח אשה ליהוה
ונסכו רביעת ההין לכבש האחד
בקדש הסך נסך שכר ליהוה ואת
הכבש השני תעשה בין הערבים
כמנחת הבקר וכנסכו תעשה אשה
ריח ניחח ליהוה
וביום השבת שני כבשים בני שנה
תמימם ושני עשרנים סלת מנחה
בלולה בשמן ונסכו עלת שבת
בשבתו על עלת התמיד ונסכה
ובראשי חדשיכם תקריבו עלה
ליהוה פרים בני בקר שנים ואיל
אחד כבשים בני שנה שבעה
תמימם ושלשה עשרנים סלת
מנחה בלולה בשמן לפר האחד
ושני עשרנים סלת מנחה בלולה
בשמן לאיל האחד ועשרן עשרון
סלת מנחה בלולה בשמן לכבש
האחד עלה ריח ניחח אשה
ליהוה ונסכיהם חצי ההין יהיה לפר
ושלישת ההין לאיל ורביעת ההין
לכבש יין זאת עלת חדש בחדשו
לחדשי השנה ושעיר עזים אחד
לחטאת ליהוה על עלת התמיד
יעשה ונסכו ובחדש
הראשון בארבעה עשר יום לחדש
פסח ליהוה ובחמשה עשר יום
לחדש הזה חג שבעת ימים מצות

48

9. וּבְיוֹם֙ הַשַּׁבָּ֔ת

שְׁנֵֽי־כְבָשִׂ֥ים בְּנֵֽי־שָׁנָ֖ה תְּמִימִ֑ם

וּשְׁנֵ֣י עֶשְׂרֹנִ֗ים

סֹ֤לֶת מִנְחָה֙

בְּלוּלָ֥ה בַשֶּׁ֖מֶן וְנִסְכּֽוֹ׃

10. עֹלַ֥ת שַׁבַּ֖ת בְּשַׁבַּתּ֑וֹ

עַל־עֹלַ֥ת הַתָּמִ֖יד וְנִסְכָּֽהּ׃

11. וּבְרָאשֵׁי֙ חָדְשֵׁיכֶ֔ם

תַּקְרִ֥יבוּ עֹלָ֖ה לַיהֹוָ֑ה

פָּרִ֨ים בְּנֵֽי־בָקָ֤ר שְׁנַ֙יִם֙ וְאַ֣יִל אֶחָ֔ד

כְּבָשִׂ֧ים בְּנֵֽי־שָׁנָ֛ה

שִׁבְעָ֖ה תְּמִימִֽם׃

12. וּשְׁלֹשָׁ֣ה עֶשְׂרֹנִ֗ים

סֹ֤לֶת מִנְחָה֙ בְּלוּלָ֣ה בַשֶּׁ֔מֶן

לַפָּ֖ר הָאֶחָ֑ד

וּשְׁנֵ֣י עֶשְׂרֹנִ֗ים

סֹ֤לֶת מִנְחָה֙ בְּלוּלָ֣ה בַשֶּׁ֔מֶן

לָאַ֖יִל הָאֶחָֽד׃

13. וְעִשָּׂרֹ֤ן עִשָּׂרוֹן֙

סֹ֤לֶת מִנְחָה֙ בְּלוּלָ֣ה בַשֶּׁ֔מֶן

לַכֶּ֖בֶשׂ הָאֶחָ֑ד

עֹלָ֣ה רֵ֣יחַ נִיחֹ֔חַ

אִשֶּׁ֖ה לַיהֹוָֽה׃

After the Torah reading, recite the following blessing.

בָּרוּךְ אַתָּה יְיָ אֱלֹהֵינוּ מֶלֶךְ הָעוֹלָם, אֲשֶׁר נָתַן לָנוּ תּוֹרַת אֱמֶת,

וְחַיֵּי עוֹלָם נָטַע בְּתוֹכֵנוּ. בָּרוּךְ אַתָּה יְיָ, נוֹתֵן הַתּוֹרָה.

We praise You, Adonai our God, Ruler of the universe,
Who planted eternal life among us by giving us a Teaching of truth.

We praise You, Adonai, the Giver of Torah.

THE HAFTARAH & ITS BLESSINGS
(YISH'AYAH / ISAIAH 66: 1-24)

OPENING BLESSING

Before the Haftarah reading, recite one of the following blessings.
Your rabbi or teacher will tell you which one is appropriate for your community.

בָּרוּךְ אַתָּה יְיָ אֱלֹהֵינוּ מֶלֶךְ הָעוֹלָם,

אֲשֶׁר בָּחַר בִּנְבִיאִים טוֹבִים,

וְרָצָה בְדִבְרֵיהֶם הַנֶּאֱמָרִים בֶּאֱמֶת.

בָּרוּךְ אַתָּה יְיָ,

הַבּוֹחֵר בַּתּוֹרָה וּבְמֹשֶׁה עַבְדּוֹ,

וּבִישְׂרָאֵל עַמּוֹ,

וּבִנְבִיאֵי הָאֱמֶת וָצֶדֶק.

בָּרוּךְ אַתָּה יְיָ אֱלֹהֵינוּ מֶלֶךְ הָעוֹלָם,

אֲשֶׁר בָּחַר בִּנְבִיאִים טוֹבִים,

וְרָצָה בְדִבְרֵיהֶם הַנֶּאֱמָרִים בֶּאֱמֶת.

בָּרוּךְ אַתָּה יְיָ,

הַבּוֹחֵר בַּתּוֹרָה וּבְמֹשֶׁה עַבְדּוֹ,

וּבִנְבִיאֵי הָאֱמֶת וָצֶדֶק.

We praise You, Adonai our God,
Ruler of the universe,
Who appointed good prophets,
and Who expected lessons of truth
in the things they said.

We praise You, Adonai,
Who chose the Torah,
and Moshe, God's servant,
and prophets of truth and righteousness.

We praise You, Adonai our God,
Ruler of the universe,
Who appointed good prophets,
and Who expected lessons of truth
in the things they said.

We praise You, Adonai,
Who chose the Torah,
and Moshe, God's servant,
and Yisra'el, God's people,
and prophets of truth and righteousness.

.1 כֹּה אָמַר יְהֹוָה

הַשָּׁמַיִם כִּסְאִי

וְהָאָרֶץ הֲדֹם רַגְלָי

אֵי־זֶה בַיִת אֲשֶׁר תִּבְנוּ־לִי

וְאֵי־זֶה מָקוֹם מְנוּחָתִי:

.2 וְאֶת־כָּל־אֵלֶּה יָדִי עָשָׂתָה

וַיִּהְיוּ כָל־אֵלֶּה נְאֻם־יְהֹוָה

וְאֶל־זֶה אַבִּיט

אֶל־עָנִי וּנְכֵה־רוּחַ

וְחָרֵד עַל־דְּבָרִי:

.3 שׁוֹחֵט הַשּׁוֹר מַכֵּה־אִישׁ

זוֹבֵחַ הַשֶּׂה עֹרֵף כֶּלֶב

מַעֲלֵה מִנְחָה דַּם־חֲזִיר

מַזְכִּיר לְבֹנָה מְבָרֵךְ אָוֶן

גַּם־הֵמָּה

בָּחֲרוּ בְּדַרְכֵיהֶם

וּבְשִׁקּוּצֵיהֶם נַפְשָׁם חָפֵצָה:

.4 גַּם־אָנִי

אֶבְחַר בְּתַעֲלֻלֵיהֶם

וּמְגוּרֹתָם אָבִיא לָהֶם

יַעַן קָרָאתִי וְאֵין עוֹנֶה

דִּבַּרְתִּי וְלֹא שָׁמֵעוּ

וַיַּעֲשׂוּ הָרַע בְּעֵינַי

וּבַאֲשֶׁר לֹא־חָפַצְתִּי בָּחָרוּ:

.5 שִׁמְעוּ דְּבַר־יְהֹוָה

הַחֲרֵדִים אֶל־דְּבָרוֹ

אָמְרוּ אֲחֵיכֶם שֹׂנְאֵיכֶם

מְנַדֵּיכֶם

לְמַעַן שְׁמִי יִכְבַּד יְהֹוָה

וְנִרְאֶה בְשִׂמְחַתְכֶם וְהֵם יֵבֹשׁוּ:

.6 קוֹל שָׁאוֹן מֵעִיר

קוֹל מֵהֵיכָל

קוֹל יְהֹוָה

מְשַׁלֵּם גְּמוּל לְאֹיְבָיו:

51

14. וּרְאִיתֶם וְשָׂשׂ לִבְּכֶם

וְעַצְמוֹתֵיכֶם כַּדֶּשֶׁא תִפְרַחְנָה

וְנוֹדְעָה יַד־יהוה אֶת־עֲבָדָיו

וְזָעַם אֶת־אֹיְבָיו:

15. כִּי־הִנֵּה יהוה בָּאֵשׁ יָבוֹא

וְכַסּוּפָה מַרְכְּבֹתָיו

לְהָשִׁיב בְּחֵמָה אַפּוֹ

וְגַעֲרָתוֹ בְּלַהֲבֵי־אֵשׁ:

16. כִּי בָאֵשׁ יהוה נִשְׁפָּט

וּבְחַרְבּוֹ אֶת־כָּל־בָּשָׂר

וְרַבּוּ חַלְלֵי יהוה:

17. הַמִּתְקַדְּשִׁים וְהַמִּטַּהֲרִים

אֶל־הַגַּנּוֹת

אַחַר אֶחָד [אַחַת] בַּתָּוֶךְ

אֹכְלֵי בְּשַׂר הַחֲזִיר

וְהַשֶּׁקֶץ וְהָעַכְבָּר

יַחְדָּו יָסֻפוּ נְאֻם־יהוה:

18. וְאָנֹכִי

מַעֲשֵׂיהֶם וּמַחְשְׁבֹתֵיהֶם

בָּאָה

לְקַבֵּץ אֶת־כָּל־הַגּוֹיִם

וְהַלְּשֹׁנוֹת

וּבָאוּ וְרָאוּ אֶת־כְּבוֹדִי:

19. וְשַׂמְתִּי בָהֶם אוֹת

וְשִׁלַּחְתִּי מֵהֶם | פְּלֵיטִים

אֶל־הַגּוֹיִם

תַּרְשִׁישׁ פּוּל וְלוּד

מֹשְׁכֵי קֶשֶׁת תֻּבַל וְיָוָן

הָאִיִּים הָרְחֹקִים

אֲשֶׁר לֹא־שָׁמְעוּ אֶת־שִׁמְעִי

וְלֹא־רָאוּ אֶת־כְּבוֹדִי

וְהִגִּידוּ אֶת־כְּבוֹדִי בַּגּוֹיִם:

7. בְּטֶרֶם תָּחִיל יָלָדָה

בְּטֶרֶם יָבוֹא חֵבֶל

לָהּ וְהִמְלִיטָה זָכָר:

8. מִי־שָׁמַע כָּזֹאת

מִי רָאָה כָּאֵלֶּה

הֲיוּחַל אֶרֶץ בְּיוֹם אֶחָד

אִם־יִוָּלֵד גּוֹי פַּעַם אֶחָת

כִּי־חָלָה

גַּם־יָלְדָה צִיּוֹן אֶת־בָּנֶיהָ:

9. הַאֲנִי אַשְׁבִּיר

וְלֹא אוֹלִיד יֹאמַר יְהֹוָה

אִם־אֲנִי הַמּוֹלִיד

וְעָצַרְתִּי אָמַר אֱלֹהָיִךְ:

10. שִׂמְחוּ אֶת־יְרוּשָׁלַםִ

וְגִילוּ בָהּ כָּל־אֹהֲבֶיהָ

שִׂישׂוּ אִתָּהּ מָשׂוֹשׂ

כָּל־הַמִּתְאַבְּלִים עָלֶיהָ:

11. לְמַעַן תִּינְקוּ וּשְׂבַעְתֶּם

מִשֹּׁד תַּנְחֻמֶיהָ

לְמַעַן תָּמֹצּוּ

וְהִתְעַנַּגְתֶּם מִזִּיז כְּבוֹדָהּ:

12. כִּי־כֹה | אָמַר יְהֹוָה

הִנְנִי נֹטֶה־אֵלֶיהָ כְּנָהָר שָׁלוֹם

וּכְנַחַל שׁוֹטֵף

כְּבוֹד גּוֹיִם וִינַקְתֶּם

עַל־צַד תִּנָּשֵׂאוּ

וְעַל־בִּרְכַּיִם תְּשָׁעֳשָׁעוּ:

13. כְּאִישׁ

אֲשֶׁר אִמּוֹ תְּנַחֲמֶנּוּ

כֵּן אָנֹכִי אֲנַחֶמְכֶם

וּבִירוּשָׁלַםִ תְּנֻחָמוּ:

20. וְהֵבִיאוּ אֶת־כָּל־אֲחֵיכֶם |

מִכָּל־הַגּוֹיִם | מִנְחָה | לַיהֹוָה

בַּסּוּסִים

וּבָרֶכֶב

וּבַצַּבִּים וּבַפְּרָדִים וּבַכִּרְכָּרוֹת

עַל הַר קָדְשִׁי

יְרוּשָׁלַ͏ִם אָמַר יְהֹוָה

כַּאֲשֶׁר יָבִיאוּ

בְּנֵי יִשְׂרָאֵל אֶת־הַמִּנְחָה

בִּכְלִי טָהוֹר בֵּית יְהֹוָה:

21. וְגַם־מֵהֶם אֶקַּח

לַכֹּהֲנִים לַלְוִיִּם אָמַר יְהֹוָה:

22. כִּי כַאֲשֶׁר הַשָּׁמַיִם הַחֳדָשִׁים

וְהָאָרֶץ הַחֲדָשָׁה

אֲשֶׁר אֲנִי עֹשֶׂה

עֹמְדִים לְפָנַי נְאֻם־יְהֹוָה

כֵּן

יַעֲמֹד זַרְעֲכֶם וְשִׁמְכֶם:

---

23. וְהָיָה

מִדֵּי־חֹדֶשׁ בְּחָדְשׁוֹ

וּמִדֵּי שַׁבָּת בְּשַׁבַּתּוֹ

יָבוֹא כָל־בָּשָׂר

לְהִשְׁתַּחֲוֹת לְפָנַי אָמַר יְהֹוָה:

24. וְיָצְאוּ וְרָאוּ בְּפִגְרֵי הָאֲנָשִׁים

הַפֹּשְׁעִים בִּי

כִּי תוֹלַעְתָּם

לֹא תָמוּת

וְאִשָּׁם לֹא תִכְבֶּה

וְהָיוּ דֵרָאוֹן לְכָל־בָּשָׂר:

וְהָיָה

מִדֵּי־חֹדֶשׁ בְּחָדְשׁוֹ

וּמִדֵּי שַׁבָּת בְּשַׁבַּתּוֹ

יָבוֹא כָל־בָּשָׂר

לְהִשְׁתַּחֲוֹת לְפָנַי אָמַר יְהֹוָה:

CLOSING BLESSINGS

After the Haftarah reading, four blessings are recited. Note that there are choices for some of them. Your rabbi or teacher will tell you which ones are appropriate for your community.

בָּרוּךְ אַתָּה יְיָ אֱלֹהֵינוּ מֶלֶךְ הָעוֹלָם, צוּר כָּל הָעוֹלָמִים, צַדִּיק בְּכָל הַדּוֹרוֹת,

הָאֵל הַנֶּאֱמָן הָאוֹמֵר וְעֹשֶׂה, הַמְדַבֵּר וּמְקַיֵּם, שֶׁכָּל דְּבָרָיו אֱמֶת וָצֶדֶק.

נֶאֱמָן אַתָּה הוּא יְיָ אֱלֹהֵינוּ, וְנֶאֱמָנִים דְּבָרֶיךָ,

וְדָבָר אֶחָד מִדְּבָרֶיךָ אָחוֹר לֹא יָשׁוּב רֵיקָם, כִּי אֵל מֶלֶךְ נֶאֱמָן וְרַחֲמָן אָתָּה.

בָּרוּךְ אַתָּה יְיָ, הָאֵל הַנֶּאֱמָן בְּכָל דְּבָרָיו.

We praise You, Adonai our God, Ruler of the universe, Creator of all the worlds,
righteous in every generation. The faithful God Who does what God says,
Who speaks and fulfills it, Whose every word is true and just.

Adonai our God, You are faithful, Your words are faithful,
and nothing You say ever goes unfulfilled. You are a faithful and merciful God and Ruler.
We praise You, Adonai, the God who is faithful in every word.

רַחֵם עַל צִיּוֹן כִּי הִיא בֵּית חַיֵּינוּ,	רַחֵם עַל צִיּוֹן כִּי הִיא בֵּית חַיֵּינוּ,
וּלְעַמְּךָ יִשְׂרָאֵל תּוֹשִׁיעַ	וְלַעֲלוּבַת נֶפֶשׁ תּוֹשִׁיעַ
בִּמְהֵרָה בְיָמֵינוּ.	בִּמְהֵרָה בְיָמֵינוּ.
בָּרוּךְ אַתָּה יְיָ, מְשַׂמֵּחַ צִיּוֹן בְּבָנֶיהָ.	בָּרוּךְ אַתָּה יְיָ, מְשַׂמֵּחַ צִיּוֹן בְּבָנֶיהָ.
Show compassion for Tzion, for she is our lifelong home. Redeem Your people Israel soon and in our lifetime.	Show compassion for Tzion, for she is our lifelong home. Redeem her distressed spirit soon and in our lifetime.
We praise You, Adonai, Who enables Tzion to rejoice with her children.	We praise you, Adonai, Who enables Tzion to rejoice with her children.

שַׂמְּחֵֽנוּ, יְיָ אֱלֹהֵֽינוּ,

בְּאֵלִיָּֽהוּ הַנָּבִיא עַבְדֶּֽךָ,

וּבְמַלְכוּת בֵּית דָּוִד מְשִׁיחֶֽךָ.

בִּמְהֵרָה יָבֹא וְיָגֵל לִבֵּֽנוּ,

עַל כִּסְאוֹ לֹא יֵֽשֶׁב זָר,

וְלֹא יִנְחֲלוּ עוֹד אֲחֵרִים אֶת כְּבוֹדוֹ,

כִּי בְשֵׁם קָדְשְׁךָ נִשְׁבַּֽעְתָּ לּוֹ

שֶׁלֹּא יִכְבֶּה נֵרוֹ לְעוֹלָם וָעֶד.

בָּרוּךְ אַתָּה יְיָ, מָגֵן דָּוִד.

שַׂמְּחֵֽנוּ, יְיָ אֱלֹהֵֽינוּ,

בְּאֵלִיָּֽהוּ הַנָּבִיא עַבְדֶּֽךָ,

בִּמְהֵרָה יָבֹא וְיָגֵל לִבֵּֽנוּ.

וְהֵשִׁיב לֵב אָבוֹת עַל בָּנִים

וְלֵב בָּנִים עַל אֲבוֹתָם,

וּבֵיתְךָ בֵּית תְּפִילָה יִקָּרֵא לְכָל הָעַמִּים.

בָּרוּךְ אַתָּה יְיָ, מֵבִיא שָׁלוֹם לָעַד.

Adonai our God,
grant us joy in Eliyahu Your prophet and
servant. Come soon to lift our hearts.
Turn the hearts of parents to their children,
and the hearts of children to their parents.
May Your House be called
a House of Prayer for all nations.
We praise You, Adonai,
Who brings peace for all time.

Adonai our God,
grant us joy in Eliyahu Your prophet
and servant, and in the reign of the dynasty
of David, Your anointed king.
May he come soon and lift our hearts.
Let no stranger sit on his throne.
Let others no longer inherit his glory,
for You swore to him by Your holy Name
that his light would never go out.
We praise You, Adonai,
Shield of David.

עַל הַתּוֹרָה, וְעַל הָעֲבוֹדָה, וְעַל הַנְּבִיאִים, וְעַל יוֹם הַשַּׁבָּת הַזֶּה,

שֶׁנָּתַתָּ לָנוּ, יְיָ אֱלֹהֵינוּ, לִקְדֻשָּׁה וְלִמְנוּחָה, לְכָבוֹד וּלְתִפְאָרֶת.

עַל הַכֹּל, יְיָ אֱלֹהֵינוּ, אֲנַחְנוּ מוֹדִים לָךְ, וּמְבָרְכִים אוֹתָךְ,

יִתְבָּרַךְ שִׁמְךָ בְּפִי כָּל חַי תָּמִיד לְעוֹלָם וָעֶד.

בָּרוּךְ אַתָּה יְיָ, מְקַדֵּשׁ הַשַּׁבָּת.

For the Torah, for our worship, for the prophets, for today's Shabbat that
You, Adonai our God, gave us for holiness, rest, glory, and wonder:
for everything, Adonai our God, we thank You and praise You.
May the lips of every living thing glorify Your Name forever.

We praise You, Adonai, Who makes Shabbat holy.

SHABBAT ZAHOR

Why is this Shabbat different from other Shabbats?

In the six weeks before Pesah, there are five special Shabbats called *Shekalim*, *Zahor*, *Parah*, *Ha-Hodesh*, and *Ha-Gadol*. The first four are called the אַרְבַּע פָּרְשִׁיוֹת ("four portions"). They feature special *Maftir* and *Haftarah* readings that relate to events in the Jewish calendar. On these days, the usual *Parashah* is read from the Torah, but the usual *Maftir* and *Haftarah* are replaced by the readings for the special day. The fifth special Shabbat, *Ha-Gadol*, always falls on the Shabbat right before Pesah. It features a special *Haftarah* that connects to... you guessed it — Pesah! It all works like this:

	Special Maftir	Special Haftarah	Why we read it
Shekalim	Shemot / Exodus 30: 11-16	2 Melahim / Kings 11: 17 to 12: 17 or 12: 1-17	In Ye Olden Dayes, every adult male paid a half-shekel tax to the Bayt Ha-Mikdash (Temple in Jerusalem) on the first day of Nisan. One month before that, at the beginning of Adar, a reminder about the tax was sent out to the people. *Shabbat Shekalim* is a memory of that reminder.
Zahor	Devarim / Deuteronomy 25: 17-19	I Shemu'el / Samuel 15: 1-34 or 15: 2-34	*Shabbat Zahor* is always read on the Shabbat before Purim. It's a reminder about the command to destroy the tribe of Amalek, who were a deadly enemy of our ancient cousins'. Haman (the villain from Purim) was a descendant of Amalek.
Parah	Ba-Midbar / Numbers 19: 1-22	Yehezk'el / Ezekiel 36: 16-38 or 36: 16-36	In Ye Olden Dayes, the altar in the Bayt Ha-Mikdash was purified in preparation for Pesah. The purification ceremony involved sacrificing a cow from a breed that was brown-red in color. *Shabbat Parah* is a memory of that ceremony.
Ha-Hodesh	Shemot / Exodus 12: 1-20	Yehezk'el / Ezekiel 45: 16 to 46: 18 or 45: 18 to 46: 15	*Shabbat Ha-Hodesh* is always read right before the start of Nisan, which is the month of Pesah. It's a reminder that Rosh Hodesh Nisan was originally the new year (not Rosh Ha-Shanah), and we review the laws of Pesah in preparation for the festival.
Ha-Gadol	None!	Mal'ahi / Malachi 3:4 - 3:24	Mal'ahi talks about restoring the proper worship of God in the Bayt Ha-Mikdash. God will send Eliyahu (Elijah) to "turn the hearts" of parents to their children and the hearts of children to their parents. Shabbat Ha-Gadol connects this with Eliyahu's visit to our seders.

What's the story so far?

The time of Avraham, Sarah, and the first family of Yisra'el has long since passed. After a long exile in Mitzra'im (Egypt), God and Moshe bring the nation of Yisra'el to Cana'an (Israel). Under the leadership of Yehoshu'a, they regain control over their ancient homeland, but peace is elusive. For more than a century, the tribes squabble among themselves. Finally, warfare forces the tribes of Yisra'el to unite under a king: Sha'ul (roughly 3000-ish years ago). But Sha'ul quickly buckles under the strain of dealing with fractious tribes, listening to the prophet, Shemu'el, and jealously watching the rise of a popular young fighter named David. The books of *1 and 2 Shemu'el* explain how the people of Yisra'el went from being a collection of tribes to a full-fledged kingdom.

What can I expect from this special Shabbat?

On the Shabbat before Purim, the regular *Maftir* and *Haftarah* are replaced by the special readings for *Shabbat Zahor*. On Purim, we read *Megillat Ester* (the story of Esther). The *Megillah* follows Queen Ester and her uncle, Mordehai, as they foil the plan of Haman to kill the Jews of Persia. *Megillat Ester* identifies Haman as an Agagite, which was a clan from the tribe of Amalek. The *Maftir* and *Haftarah* for *Shabbat Zahor* describe the conflict from Ye Olden Dayes between Benay Yisra'el and Amalek. Why were these specific passages chosen for public reading right before Purim? How does *Shabbat Zahor* enhance our understanding and celebration of Purim? Explore the connections between today's *Maftir / Haftarah* and *Megillat Ester*.

And so, without further ado, on to *Shabbat Zahor*!

DEVARIM / DEUTERONOMY 25: 17-19

REMEMBER!

25: 17-19

Moshe is doing the talking here. Benay Yisra'el are waiting near the border of the Promised Land and they're about to reclaim their ancestral homeland. Before they do, Moshe gives them a huge list of reminders and to-do's (see the entire book of *Devarim / Deuteronomy*). Amalek was a tribe that lived in the Negev region, and in our small section here, Moshe reminds Benay Yisra'el of Amalek's attack after Benay Yisra'el left **Mitzra'im** (Egypt). For details, see chapter 17 in *Shemot / Exodus*.

Remember what Amalek did to you on your way out of **Mitzra'im**! Remember how Amalek attacked the people who trailed behind you — the weakest and most vulnerable among you — while you were weary and exhausted. Amalek had no fear of Elohim! In times to come, when Adonai your God gives you rest from the enemies who surround you, when you have settled comfortably in the land that Adonai your God has given you as an inheritance, you will utterly wipe out the memory of Amalek from under the heavens.

DO NOT FORGET!

1 SHEMU'EL / SAMUEL 15: 1-34 (OR 15: 2-34)

MISSION: AMALEK

15: 1-3

Shemu'el approached **Sha'ul**. "Adonai sent me to appoint you king over God's people, Yisra'el. Now listen to Adonai's Message."

I recall Amalek's actions in assaulting Yisra'el after Yisra'el came up from Mitzra'im. Go now and attack Amalek! Wipe them out completely — man and woman, infant and child, ox and sheep, camel and donkey!

15: 4-9

Sha'ul mustered his forces at Tela'im — 200,000 infantry including 10,000 from the tribe of Yehudah. Sha'ul led them to the valley near Amalek's main town, where they prepared to attack. Sha'ul sent a message to the **Kenites**:

"Get away from the Amalekites so I don't destroy you along with them! I give you this chance because you were merciful to Benay Yisra'el when they came up from Mitzra'im."

So the Kenites abandoned the Amalekites.

Sha'ul attacked Amalek in a battle that ranged from Havilah to Shur near the Mitzra'imite border. He captured the Amalekite king, **Agag**, and annihilated the rest of the people. Sha'ul and his troops spared Agag and the best of the livestock. They only destroyed what had no value.

Shemu'el was a prophet of God. A "prophet" is someone who has a special gift for communicating God's inspiring message to the people and leaders of Yisra'el. Before there was a kingdom, Yisra'el was organized into tribes. These tribes often squabbled, but they sometimes came together under the leadership of a charismatic chieftain. Shemu'el was the last of these chieftains. (The adventures of the chieftains who lived before Shemu'el are recorded in the book of *Shoftim / Judges*.)

The book of *Shemu'el* follows the lives of Shemu'el and the first two kings of Yisra'el: **Sha'ul** and David. Sha'ul was unable to unite the tribes of Yisra'el for very long, and he died in battle against the Pelishtim (Philistines). His famous general, David, was appointed king after him. David was wildly successful, uniting the tribes and expanding the borders of the kingdom of Yisra'el to include most of the neighboring peoples. David established Jerusalem as the eternal capital of the nation of Yisra'el (3000-ish years ago) and he established his family as the ruling dynasty.

Wipe them out completely: To many modern readers, it looks like God is commanding a genocide, which is exactly what people like Adolf Hitler tried to do to us. It hardly seems fair or ethical — especially for the children and animals. In Ye Olden Dayes, this kind of total destruction was occasionally used by kingdoms to demonstrate their power and to warn other nations to do what they're told. From this perspective, the command to destroy Amalek is consistent with the way warfare was sometimes done. For a long time, Jewish tradition has understood "Amalek" to represent our worst impulses so that "wiping out Amalek" can be seen on a more metaphorical level. Your rabbi / teacher can help you explore these ideas.

Kenites: This tribal group lived in the same general area as Amalek and Yehudah. Moshe's father-in-law was a Kenite and they were considered allies of Yehudah. For more, see the first chapter of the book of *Shoftim / Judges*.

Agag: Does this name look familiar? Hint: check out the third chapter of *Megillat Ester*. Your rabbi / teacher can help you explore the thematic connections between this *Haftarah* and Purim.

15:10-15

Then Shemu'el received a Message from Adonai.

I regret crowning Sha'ul king. By failing to fulfill My orders, he has turned his back on Me.

Shemu'el was upset by this and he cried out to Adonai all night. He got up early the next morning to summon Sha'ul, but a messenger told him that Sha'ul had gone to **Carmel** to set up a victory monument before heading down to **Gilgal**.

When Shemu'el came to Sha'ul, the king called out, "I bless you, who comes from Adonai! I've carried out Adonai's orders!"

"Oh? So what's all the noise from sheep and cattle I hear?" demanded Shemu'el.

"They brought them here from Amalek," answered Sha'ul. "The people kept the best of the livestock in order to make them a sacrifice to Adonai your God. We destroyed the rest."

15:16-23

"Just a minute," replied Shemu'el. "Let me tell you about Adonai's Message to me last night."

"Go on."

Shemu'el shook his head sadly. "You may seem small to yourself, but you're the head of Yisra'el's tribes, are you not? Did Adonai not anoint you king over Yisra'el? Adonai sent you on a mission to destroy Amalek's corruption and to continue fighting until they were completely wiped out. Why then did you ignore Adonai's order by seizing all this plunder? This is unacceptable to Adonai!"

"I *have* fulfilled Adonai's orders," defended Sha'ul. "I did what Adonai told me. I captured king Agag of Amalek and destroyed the rest of Amalek. It was the troops who took all the spoils — the sheep, cattle, and the most valuable possessions — to make a huge sacrifice to Adonai your God here at Gilgal."

"Does Adonai take as much pleasure in fiery offerings as in people following God's Orders? It's better to obey than to worry about the fatty parts of livestock! This kind of failure is like the horrid crime of

Carmel...Gilgal: These were towns in the tribal territories of Yehudah and Binyamin in the south-central area of modern-day Israel. It's a different "Carmel" than the mountain in Israel's north where the city of Haifa is now.

Witchcraft: In Ye Olden Dayes, the practice of any kind of magic like witchcraft, necromancy, etc., was considered to be a major crime against God. What was the big deal, you ask? Sorcery was often connected to the blood magic and human sacrifice that were practiced by Yisra'el's enemies, and which were explicitly forbidden by God. For more details, see chapter 18 in the book of *Devarim / Deuteronomy*.

Terafim: These were small idols that were used by magicians and witches to see into the future.

To many readers, Shemu'el's reaction seems a bit excessive. Okay, so Sha'ul didn't do *exactly* what he was told, but he got most of it right, didn't he? This may be true, but it misses the point. When a parent or a teacher tells you to do something, how do you think they feel when you only do part of what you asked to do? Should police officers get to decide how much of the law to enforce? When national leaders behave as if laws only apply to them when they feel like it, what effect does it have on the country? Your rabbi / teacher can help you to explore the possible reasons for Shemu'el's and God's harsh reaction to Sha'ul.

witchcraft! This kind of insolence is like the crime of consulting **terafim**! Since you've rejected Adonai's divine authority, Adonai has rejected your royal authority!"

15:24-31

"I've made a terrible mistake," admitted Sha'ul. "I went against Adonai's orders and against yours. It's just that I was afraid of the troops so I did as they asked! Please, forgive my error and come back with me so I can worship Adonai."

Shemu'el shook his head. "I can't come back with you. You rejected Adonai's authority and Adonai has rejected your kingship over Yisra'el."

As Shemu'el turned away, Sha'ul grabbed the edge of the prophet's robe and it tore. Looking back, Shemu'el announced, "Adonai has torn the kingdom of Yisra'el from you and given it to a man worthier than you! The Glorious One of Yisra'el isn't like a human being who flip-flops!"

"I made a mistake," repeated Sha'ul. "Please, let me save face in front of the elders of my people and before all of Yisra'el. Come back with me so I can worship Adonai your God."

Shemu'el turned away again from Sha'ul. Then the king worshipped Adonai.

15:32-34

"Bring me the Amalekite king, Agag!" demanded Shemu'el.

Agag came stumbling out. "Ah, my bitter death is here!" he called out.

"Just as your sword has made countless women childless, may your mother now become childless among women!" pronounced Shemu'el.

Shemu'el cut Agag down in Adonai's Presence there in Gilgal.

Shemu'el then returned to his home in Ramah while Sha'ul went up to Giv'at-Sha'ul.

THE MAFTIR & ITS BLESSINGS
(DEVARIM / DEUTERONOMY 25: 17-19)

Before the Torah reading, recite one of the following blessings. Your rabbi or teacher will tell you which one is appropriate for your community.

You call out:

בָּרְכוּ אֶת יְיָ הַמְבֹרָךְ.

The congregation responds:

בָּרוּךְ יְיָ הַמְבֹרָךְ לְעוֹלָם וָעֶד.

You say it back to them:

בָּרוּךְ יְיָ הַמְבֹרָךְ לְעוֹלָם וָעֶד.

You continue:

בָּרוּךְ אַתָּה יְיָ אֱלֹהֵינוּ מֶלֶךְ הָעוֹלָם,

אֲשֶׁר קֵרְבָנוּ לַעֲבוֹדָתוֹ

וְנָתַן לָנוּ אֶת תּוֹרָתוֹ.

בָּרוּךְ אַתָּה יְיָ, נוֹתֵן הַתּוֹרָה.

Let us praise Adonai,
the Blessed One!

Let Adonai, the Blessed One,
be praised forever!

We praise You, Adonai our God,
Ruler of the universe,
Who drew us close to God's Work
and gave us God's Torah.

We praise You, Adonai,
the Giver of Torah.

You call out:

בָּרְכוּ אֶת יְיָ הַמְבֹרָךְ.

The congregation responds:

בָּרוּךְ יְיָ הַמְבֹרָךְ לְעוֹלָם וָעֶד.

You say it back to them:

בָּרוּךְ יְיָ הַמְבֹרָךְ לְעוֹלָם וָעֶד.

You continue:

בָּרוּךְ אַתָּה יְיָ אֱלֹהֵינוּ מֶלֶךְ הָעוֹלָם,

אֲשֶׁר בָּחַר בָּנוּ מִכָּל הָעַמִּים

וְנָתַן לָנוּ אֶת תּוֹרָתוֹ.

בָּרוּךְ אַתָּה יְיָ, נוֹתֵן הַתּוֹרָה.

Let us praise Adonai,
the Blessed One!

Let Adonai, the Blessed One,
be praised forever!

We praise You, Adonai our God,
Ruler of the universe,
Who chose us from all the nations
to be given God's Torah.

We praise You, Adonai,
the Giver of Torah.

גְדוּלָה וּקְטַנָּה לֹא יִהְיֶה לְךָ בְּבֵיתְךָ
אֵיפָה וְאֵיפָה גְדוּלָה וּקְטַנָּה אֶבֶן
שְׁלֵמָה וָצֶדֶק יִהְיֶה לָּךְ אֵיפָה שְׁלֵמָה
וָצֶדֶק יִהְיֶה לָּךְ לְמַעַן יַאֲרִיכוּ יָמֶיךָ עַל
הָאֲדָמָה אֲשֶׁר יְהוָה אֱלֹהֶיךָ נֹתֵן לָךְ כִּי
תוֹעֲבַת יְהוָה אֱלֹהֶיךָ כֹּל עֹשֵׂה אֵלֶּה
כֹּל עֹשֵׂה עָוֶל

זָכוֹר אֵת אֲשֶׁר עָשָׂה לְךָ עֲמָלֵק בַּדֶּרֶךְ
בְּצֵאתְכֶם מִמִּצְרָיִם אֲשֶׁר קָרְךָ בַּדֶּרֶךְ
וַיְזַנֵּב בְּךָ כָּל הַנֶּחֱשָׁלִים אַחֲרֶיךָ וְאַתָּה
עָיֵף וְיָגֵעַ וְלֹא יָרֵא אֱלֹהִים וְהָיָה
בְּהָנִיחַ יְהוָה אֱלֹהֶיךָ לְךָ מִכָּל אֹיְבֶיךָ
מִסָּבִיב בָּאָרֶץ אֲשֶׁר יְהוָה אֱלֹהֶיךָ נֹתֵן
לְךָ נַחֲלָה לְרִשְׁתָּהּ תִּמְחֶה אֶת זֵכֶר
עֲמָלֵק מִתַּחַת הַשָּׁמַיִם לֹא תִּשְׁכָּח

וְהָיָה כִּי תָבוֹא אֶל הָאָרֶץ אֲשֶׁר יְהוָה
אֱלֹהֶיךָ נֹתֵן לְךָ נַחֲלָה וִירִשְׁתָּהּ וְיָשַׁבְתָּ
בָּהּ וְלָקַחְתָּ מֵרֵאשִׁית כָּל פְּרִי הָאֲדָמָה
אֲשֶׁר תָּבִיא מֵאַרְצְךָ אֲשֶׁר יְהוָה
אֱלֹהֶיךָ נֹתֵן לָךְ וְשַׂמְתָּ בַטֶּנֶא וְהָלַכְתָּ
אֶל הַמָּקוֹם אֲשֶׁר יִבְחַר יְהוָה אֱלֹהֶיךָ
לְשַׁכֵּן שְׁמוֹ שָׁם וּבָאתָ אֶל הַכֹּהֵן אֲשֶׁר
יִהְיֶה בַּיָּמִים הָהֵם וְאָמַרְתָּ אֵלָיו
הִגַּדְתִּי הַיּוֹם לַיהוָה אֱלֹהֶיךָ כִּי בָאתִי
אֶל הָאָרֶץ אֲשֶׁר נִשְׁבַּע יְהוָה לַאֲבֹתֵינוּ
לָתֶת לָנוּ וְלָקַח הַכֹּהֵן הַטֶּנֶא מִיָּדֶךָ
וְהִנִּיחוֹ לִפְנֵי מִזְבַּח יְהוָה אֱלֹהֶיךָ

17. זָכוֹר

אֵת

אֲשֶׁר־עָשָׂה לְךָ עֲמָלֵק

בַּדֶּרֶךְ בְּצֵאתְכֶם מִמִּצְרָיִם:

18. אֲשֶׁר קָרְךָ בַּדֶּרֶךְ

וַיְזַנֵּב בְּךָ כָּל־הַנֶּחֱשָׁלִים אַחֲרֶיךָ

וְאַתָּה עָיֵף וְיָגֵעַ

וְלֹא יָרֵא אֱלֹהִים:

19. וְהָיָה

בְּהָנִיחַ יְהוָה אֱלֹהֶיךָ ׀ לְךָ

מִכָּל־אֹיְבֶיךָ מִסָּבִיב

בָּאָרֶץ

אֲשֶׁר יְהוָה־אֱלֹהֶיךָ

נֹתֵן לְךָ נַחֲלָה לְרִשְׁתָּהּ

תִּמְחֶה אֶת־זֵכֶר עֲמָלֵק

מִתַּחַת הַשָּׁמָיִם

לֹא תִּשְׁכָּח:

TURN THE PAGE FOR THE CLOSING BLESSING.

After the Torah reading, recite the following blessing.

בָּרוּךְ אַתָּה יְיָ אֱלֹהֵינוּ מֶלֶךְ הָעוֹלָם, אֲשֶׁר נָתַן לָנוּ תּוֹרַת אֱמֶת,

וְחַיֵּי עוֹלָם נָטַע בְּתוֹכֵנוּ. בָּרוּךְ אַתָּה יְיָ, נוֹתֵן הַתּוֹרָה.

We praise You, Adonai our God, Ruler of the universe,
Who planted eternal life among us by giving us a Teaching of truth.

We praise You, Adonai, the Giver of Torah.

THE HAFTARAH & ITS BLESSINGS (1 SHEMU'EL / SAMUEL 15: 1-34 OR 15: 2-34)

Before the Haftarah reading, recite one of the following blessings.
Your rabbi or teacher will tell you which one is appropriate for your community.

בָּרוּךְ אַתָּה יְיָ אֱלֹהֵֽינוּ מֶֽלֶךְ הָעוֹלָם,

אֲשֶׁר בָּחַר בִּנְבִיאִים טוֹבִים,

וְרָצָה בְדִבְרֵיהֶם הַנֶּאֱמָרִים בֶּאֱמֶת.

בָּרוּךְ אַתָּה יְיָ,

הַבּוֹחֵר בַּתּוֹרָה וּבְמֹשֶׁה עַבְדּוֹ,

וּבְיִשְׂרָאֵל עַמּוֹ,

וּבִנְבִיאֵי הָאֱמֶת וָצֶֽדֶק.

We praise You, Adonai our God,
Ruler of the universe,
Who appointed good prophets,
and Who expected lessons of truth
in the things they said.

We praise You, Adonai,
Who chose the Torah,
and Moshe, God's servant,
and Yisra'el, God's people,
and prophets of truth and righteousness.

בָּרוּךְ אַתָּה יְיָ אֱלֹהֵֽינוּ מֶֽלֶךְ הָעוֹלָם,

אֲשֶׁר בָּחַר בִּנְבִיאִים טוֹבִים,

וְרָצָה בְדִבְרֵיהֶם הַנֶּאֱמָרִים בֶּאֱמֶת.

בָּרוּךְ אַתָּה יְיָ,

הַבּוֹחֵר בַּתּוֹרָה וּבְמֹשֶׁה עַבְדּוֹ,

וּבִנְבִיאֵי הָאֱמֶת וָצֶֽדֶק.

We praise You, Adonai our God,
Ruler of the universe,
Who appointed good prophets,
and Who expected lessons of truth
in the things they said.

We praise You, Adonai,
Who chose the Torah,
and Moshe, God's servant,
and prophets of truth and righteousness.

67

8. וַיִּתְפֹּשׂ
אֶת־אֲגַג מֶלֶךְ־עֲמָלֵק חָי
וְאֶת־כָּל־הָעָם הֶחֱרִים לְפִי־חָרֶב:

9. וַיַּחְמֹל שָׁאוּל וְהָעָם עַל־אֲגָג
וְעַל־מֵיטַב הַצֹּאן
וְהַבָּקָר וְהַמִּשְׁנִים וְעַל־הַכָּרִים
וְעַל־כָּל־הַטּוֹב
וְלֹא אָבוּ הַחֲרִימָם
וְכָל־הַמְּלָאכָה
נְמִבְזָה וְנָמֵס אֹתָהּ הֶחֱרִימוּ:

10. וַיְהִי דְבַר־יְהוָֹה
אֶל־שְׁמוּאֵל לֵאמֹר:

11. נִחַמְתִּי
כִּי־הִמְלַכְתִּי אֶת־שָׁאוּל לְמֶלֶךְ
כִּי־שָׁב מֵאַחֲרַי
וְאֶת־דְּבָרַי לֹא הֵקִים
וַיִּחַר לִשְׁמוּאֵל
וַיִּזְעַק אֶל־יְהוָה כָּל־הַלָּיְלָה:

12. וַיַּשְׁכֵּם שְׁמוּאֵל
לִקְרַאת שָׁאוּל בַּבֹּקֶר
וַיֻּגַּד לִשְׁמוּאֵל לֵאמֹר
בָּא־שָׁאוּל הַכַּרְמֶלָה
וְהִנֵּה מַצִּיב לוֹ יָד
וַיִּסֹּב וַיַּעֲבֹר
וַיֵּרֶד הַגִּלְגָּל:

13. וַיָּבֹא שְׁמוּאֵל אֶל־שָׁאוּל
וַיֹּאמֶר לוֹ שָׁאוּל
בָּרוּךְ אַתָּה לַיהוָה
הֲקִימֹתִי אֶת־דְּבַר יְהוָה:

14. וַיֹּאמֶר שְׁמוּאֵל
וּמֶה
קוֹל־הַצֹּאן הַזֶּה בְּאָזְנָי
וְקוֹל הַבָּקָר
אֲשֶׁר אָנֹכִי שֹׁמֵעַ:

68

1. וַיֹּ֤אמֶר שְׁמוּאֵל֙ אֶל־שָׁא֔וּל

אֹתִ֨י שָׁלַ֤ח יהוה֙ לִמְשָׁחֲךָ֣ לְמֶ֔לֶךְ

עַל־עַמּ֖וֹ עַל־יִשְׂרָאֵ֑ל

וְעַתָּ֣ה שְׁמַ֔ע

לְק֖וֹל דִּבְרֵ֥י יהוה׃

2. כֹּ֤ה אָמַר֙ יהוה צְבָא֔וֹת

פָּקַ֕דְתִּי

אֵ֛ת

אֲשֶׁר־עָשָׂ֥ה עֲמָלֵ֖ק לְיִשְׂרָאֵ֑ל

אֲשֶׁר־שָׂ֥ם לוֹ֙ בַּדֶּ֔רֶךְ

בַּעֲלֹת֖וֹ מִמִּצְרָֽיִם׃

3. עַתָּה֩ לֵ֨ךְ וְהִכִּיתָ֜ה אֶת־עֲמָלֵ֗ק

וְהַחֲרַמְתֶּם֙ אֶת־כָּל־אֲשֶׁר־ל֔וֹ

וְלֹ֥א תַחְמֹ֖ל עָלָ֑יו

וְהֵמַתָּ֞ה

מֵאִ֣ישׁ עַד־אִשָּׁ֗ה

מֵעֹלֵל֙ וְעַד־יוֹנֵ֔ק

מִשּׁ֣וֹר וְעַד־שֶׂ֔ה

מִגָּמָ֖ל וְעַד־חֲמֽוֹר׃

4. וַיְשַׁמַּ֤ע שָׁאוּל֙ אֶת־הָעָ֔ם

וַֽיִּפְקְדֵ֖ם בַּטְּלָאִ֑ים

מָאתַ֤יִם אֶ֙לֶף֙ רַגְלִ֔י

וַעֲשֶׂ֥רֶת אֲלָפִ֖ים אֶת־אִ֥ישׁ יְהוּדָֽה׃

5. וַיָּבֹ֥א שָׁא֖וּל עַד־עִ֣יר עֲמָלֵ֑ק

וַיָּ֖רֶב בַּנָּֽחַל׃

6. וַיֹּ֣אמֶר שָׁא֣וּל אֶל־הַקֵּינִ֡י

לְכוּ֩ סֻּ֨רוּ רְד֜וּ מִתּ֣וֹךְ עֲמָלֵקִ֗י

פֶּן־אֹֽסִפְךָ֙ עִמּ֔וֹ

וְאַתָּ֞ה

עָשִׂ֤יתָה חֶ֙סֶד֙

עִם־כָּל־בְּנֵ֣י יִשְׂרָאֵ֔ל

בַּעֲלוֹתָ֖ם מִמִּצְרָ֑יִם

וַיָּ֥סַר קֵינִ֖י מִתּ֥וֹךְ עֲמָלֵֽק׃

7. וַיַּ֥ךְ שָׁא֖וּל אֶת־עֲמָלֵ֑ק

מֵֽחֲוִילָה֙ בּוֹאֲךָ֣ שׁ֔וּר

אֲשֶׁ֖ר עַל־פְּנֵ֥י מִצְרָֽיִם׃

69

21. וַיִּקַּח הָעָם מֵהַשָּׁלָל
צֹאן וּבָקָר רֵאשִׁית הַחֵרֶם
לִזְבֹּחַ
לַיהוָה אֱלֹהֶיךָ בַּגִּלְגָּל:

22. וַיֹּאמֶר שְׁמוּאֵל
הַחֵפֶץ לַיהוָה בְּעֹלוֹת וּזְבָחִים
כִּשְׁמֹעַ בְּקוֹל יְהוָה
הִנֵּה שְׁמֹעַ מִזֶּבַח טוֹב
לְהַקְשִׁיב מֵחֵלֶב אֵילִים:

23. כִּי חַטַּאת־קֶסֶם מֶרִי
וְאָוֶן וּתְרָפִים הַפְצַר
יַעַן
מָאַסְתָּ אֶת־דְּבַר יְהוָה
וַיִּמְאָסְךָ מִמֶּלֶךְ:

24. וַיֹּאמֶר שָׁאוּל אֶל־שְׁמוּאֵל חָטָאתִי
כִּי־עָבַרְתִּי אֶת־פִּי־יְהוָה
וְאֶת־דְּבָרֶיךָ
כִּי יָרֵאתִי אֶת־הָעָם
וָאֶשְׁמַע בְּקוֹלָם:

25. וְעַתָּה
שָׂא נָא אֶת־חַטָּאתִי
וְשׁוּב עִמִּי
וְאֶשְׁתַּחֲוֶה לַיהוָה:

26. וַיֹּאמֶר שְׁמוּאֵל אֶל־שָׁאוּל
לֹא אָשׁוּב עִמָּךְ
כִּי מָאַסְתָּה אֶת־דְּבַר יְהוָה
וַיִּמְאָסְךָ יְהוָה
מִהְיוֹת מֶלֶךְ עַל־יִשְׂרָאֵל:

27. וַיִּסֹּב שְׁמוּאֵל לָלֶכֶת
וַיַּחֲזֵק בִּכְנַף־מְעִילוֹ וַיִּקָּרַע:

15. וַיֹּאמֶר שָׁאוּל מֵעֲמָלֵקִי הֱבִיאוּם

אֲשֶׁר חָמַל הָעָם

עַל־מֵיטַב הַצֹּאן וְהַבָּקָר

לְמַעַן זְבֹחַ לַיהוָה אֱלֹהֶיךָ

וְאֶת־הַיּוֹתֵר הֶחֱרַמְנוּ:

16. וַיֹּאמֶר שְׁמוּאֵל אֶל־שָׁאוּל

הֶרֶף וְאַגִּידָה לְּךָ

אֵת אֲשֶׁר דִּבֶּר יְהוָה

אֵלַי הַלָּיְלָה

ויאמרו [וַיֹּאמֶר] לוֹ דַּבֵּר:

17. וַיֹּאמֶר שְׁמוּאֵל

הֲלוֹא

אִם־קָטֹן אַתָּה בְּעֵינֶיךָ

רֹאשׁ

שִׁבְטֵי יִשְׂרָאֵל אָתָּה

וַיִּמְשָׁחֲךָ יְהוָה

לְמֶלֶךְ עַל־יִשְׂרָאֵל:

18. וַיִּשְׁלָחֲךָ יְהוָה בְּדָרֶךְ

וַיֹּאמֶר

לֵךְ וְהַחֲרַמְתָּה

אֶת־הַחַטָּאִים אֶת־עֲמָלֵק

וְנִלְחַמְתָּ בוֹ

עַד כַּלּוֹתָם אֹתָם:

19. וְלָמָּה לֹא־שָׁמַעְתָּ בְּקוֹל יְהוָה

וַתַּעַט אֶל־הַשָּׁלָל

וַתַּעַשׂ הָרַע בְּעֵינֵי יְהוָה:

20. וַיֹּאמֶר שָׁאוּל אֶל־שְׁמוּאֵל

אֲשֶׁר שָׁמַעְתִּי בְּקוֹל יְהוָה

וָאֵלֵךְ

בַּדֶּרֶךְ אֲשֶׁר־שְׁלָחַנִי יְהוָה

וָאָבִיא

אֶת־אֲגַג מֶלֶךְ עֲמָלֵק

וְאֶת־עֲמָלֵק הֶחֱרַמְתִּי:

28. וַיֹּאמֶר אֵלָיו שְׁמוּאֵל

קָרַע יְהֹוָה

אֶת־מַמְלְכוּת יִשְׂרָאֵל

מֵעָלֶיךָ הַיּוֹם

וּנְתָנָהּ

לְרֵעֲךָ הַטּוֹב מִמֶּךָּ:

29. וְגַם נֵצַח יִשְׂרָאֵל

לֹא יְשַׁקֵּר וְלֹא יִנָּחֵם

כִּי לֹא אָדָם

הוּא לְהִנָּחֵם:

30. וַיֹּאמֶר חָטָאתִי

עַתָּה

כַּבְּדֵנִי נָא

נֶגֶד־זִקְנֵי עַמִּי וְנֶגֶד יִשְׂרָאֵל

וְשׁוּב עִמִּי

וְהִשְׁתַּחֲוֵיתִי לַיהֹוָה אֱלֹהֶיךָ:

31. וַיָּשָׁב שְׁמוּאֵל אַחֲרֵי שָׁאוּל

וַיִּשְׁתַּחוּ שָׁאוּל לַיהֹוָה:

32. וַיֹּאמֶר שְׁמוּאֵל

הַגִּישׁוּ אֵלַי

אֶת־אֲגַג מֶלֶךְ עֲמָלֵק

וַיֵּלֶךְ אֵלָיו

אֲגַג מַעֲדַנֹּת

וַיֹּאמֶר אֲגָג

אָכֵן סָר מַר־הַמָּוֶת:

33. וַיֹּאמֶר שְׁמוּאֵל

כַּאֲשֶׁר שִׁכְּלָה נָשִׁים חַרְבֶּךָ

כֵּן־תִּשְׁכַּל מִנָּשִׁים אִמֶּךָ

וַיְשַׁסֵּף שְׁמוּאֵל אֶת־אֲגָג

לִפְנֵי יְהֹוָה בַּגִּלְגָּל:

34. וַיֵּלֶךְ שְׁמוּאֵל הָרָמָתָה

וְשָׁאוּל

עָלָה אֶל־בֵּיתוֹ גִּבְעַת שָׁאוּל:

72

CLOSING BLESSINGS FOR THE HAFTARAH

After the *Haftarah* reading, four blessings are recited. Note that there are choices for some of them. Your rabbi or teacher will tell you which ones are appropriate for your community.

בָּרוּךְ אַתָּה יְיָ אֱלֹהֵינוּ מֶלֶךְ הָעוֹלָם, צוּר כָּל הָעוֹלָמִים, צַדִּיק בְּכָל הַדּוֹרוֹת,

הָאֵל הַנֶּאֱמָן הָאוֹמֵר וְעֹשֶׂה, הַמְדַבֵּר וּמְקַיֵּם, שֶׁכָּל דְּבָרָיו אֱמֶת וָצֶדֶק.

נֶאֱמָן אַתָּה הוּא יְיָ אֱלֹהֵינוּ, וְנֶאֱמָנִים דְּבָרֶיךָ,

וְדָבָר אֶחָד מִדְּבָרֶיךָ אָחוֹר לֹא יָשׁוּב רֵיקָם, כִּי אֵל מֶלֶךְ נֶאֱמָן וְרַחֲמָן אָתָּה.

בָּרוּךְ אַתָּה יְיָ, הָאֵל הַנֶּאֱמָן בְּכָל דְּבָרָיו.

We praise You, Adonai our God, Ruler of the universe, Creator of all the worlds, righteous in every generation. The faithful God Who does what God says, Who speaks and fulfills it, Whose every word is true and just.

Adonai our God, You are faithful, Your words are faithful, and nothing You say ever goes unfulfilled. You are a faithful and merciful God and Ruler. We praise You, Adonai, the God who is faithful in every word.

<table>
<tr>
<td>

רַחֵם עַל צִיּוֹן כִּי הִיא בֵּית חַיֵּינוּ,

וּלְעַמְּךָ יִשְׂרָאֵל תּוֹשִׁיעַ

בִּמְהֵרָה בְיָמֵינוּ.

בָּרוּךְ אַתָּה יְיָ, מְשַׂמֵּחַ צִיּוֹן בְּבָנֶיהָ.

</td>
<td>

רַחֵם עַל צִיּוֹן כִּי הִיא בֵּית חַיֵּינוּ,

וְלַעֲלוּבַת נֶפֶשׁ תּוֹשִׁיעַ

בִּמְהֵרָה בְיָמֵינוּ.

בָּרוּךְ אַתָּה יְיָ, מְשַׂמֵּחַ צִיּוֹן בְּבָנֶיהָ.

</td>
</tr>
<tr>
<td>

Show compassion for Tzion, for she is our lifelong home. Redeem Your people Israel soon and in our lifetime.

We praise You, Adonai, Who enables Tzion to rejoice with her children.

</td>
<td>

Show compassion for Tzion, for she is our lifelong home. Redeem her distressed spirit soon and in our lifetime.

We praise you, Adonai, Who enables Tzion to rejoice with her children.

</td>
</tr>
</table>

שַׂמְּחֵנוּ, יְיָ אֱלֹהֵינוּ,

בְּאֵלִיָּֽהוּ הַנָּבִיא עַבְדֶּֽךָ,

וּבְמַלְכוּת בֵּית דָּוִד מְשִׁיחֶֽךָ.

בִּמְהֵרָה יָבֹא וְיָגֵל לִבֵּֽנוּ,

עַל כִּסְאוֹ לֹא יֵשֵׁב זָר,

וְלֹא יִנְחֲלוּ עוֹד אֲחֵרִים אֶת כְּבוֹדוֹ,

כִּי בְשֵׁם קָדְשְׁךָ נִשְׁבַּֽעְתָּ לּוֹ

שֶׁלֹּא יִכְבֶּה נֵרוֹ לְעוֹלָם וָעֶד.

בָּרוּךְ אַתָּה יְיָ, מָגֵן דָּוִד.

שַׂמְּחֵנוּ, יְיָ אֱלֹהֵינוּ,

בְּאֵלִיָּֽהוּ הַנָּבִיא עַבְדֶּֽךָ,

בִּמְהֵרָה יָבֹא וְיָגֵל לִבֵּֽנוּ.

וְהֵשִׁיב לֵב אָבוֹת עַל בָּנִים

וְלֵב בָּנִים עַל אֲבוֹתָם,

וּבֵיתְךָ בֵּית תְּפִילָּה יִקָּרֵא לְכָל הָעַמִּים.

בָּרוּךְ אַתָּה יְיָ, מֵבִיא שָׁלוֹם לָעַד.

Adonai our God,
grant us joy in Eliyahu Your prophet and
servant. Come soon to lift our hearts.
Turn the hearts of parents to their children,
and the hearts of children to their parents.
May Your House be called
a House of Prayer for all nations.
We praise You, Adonai,
Who brings peace for all time.

Adonai our God,
grant us joy in Eliyahu Your prophet
and servant, and in the reign of the dynasty
of David, Your anointed king.
May he come soon and lift our hearts.
Let no stranger sit on his throne.
Let others no longer inherit his glory,
for You swore to him by Your holy Name
that his light would never go out.
We praise You, Adonai,
Shield of David.

עַל הַתּוֹרָה, וְעַל הָעֲבוֹדָה, וְעַל הַנְּבִיאִים, וְעַל יוֹם הַשַּׁבָּת הַזֶּה,

שֶׁנָּתַתָּ לָנוּ, יְיָ אֱלֹהֵינוּ, לִקְדֻשָּׁה וְלִמְנוּחָה, לְכָבוֹד וּלְתִפְאָרֶת.

עַל הַכֹּל, יְיָ אֱלֹהֵינוּ, אֲנַחְנוּ מוֹדִים לָךְ, וּמְבָרְכִים אוֹתָךְ,

יִתְבָּרַךְ שִׁמְךָ בְּפִי כָּל חַי תָּמִיד לְעוֹלָם וָעֶד.

בָּרוּךְ אַתָּה יְיָ, מְקַדֵּשׁ הַשַּׁבָּת.

For the Torah, for our worship, for the prophets, for today's Shabbat that
You, Adonai our God, gave us for holiness, rest, glory, and wonder:
for everything, Adonai our God, we thank You and praise You.
May the lips of every living thing glorify Your Name forever.

We praise You, Adonai, Who makes Shabbat holy.

TA'AMEI HA-MIKRA: TROP CHARTS

Let's face it: learning trop can be very difficult. Most of us are used to the idea that each musical sign represents a single tone, but with trop, most signs (*ta'amim*) represent musical phrases. To add to the difficulty, there are 28 separate trop signs — each with a unique musical phrase, and sometimes the phrasing changes depending on the combination of *ta'amim* (though very few readings contain all 28 *ta'amim*). Sure, you can find sheet music to help you out, but if you're like me and don't read music, you might wind up more confused. Oy!

I developed the charts in this section to help people like me. Most of the *ta'amim* are grouped into sequences that are used commonly in the Tanah. The grids enable the teacher and the student to chart the music as it goes higher or lower.

These charts have proven quite helpful with my own students. I hope you find them just as useful!

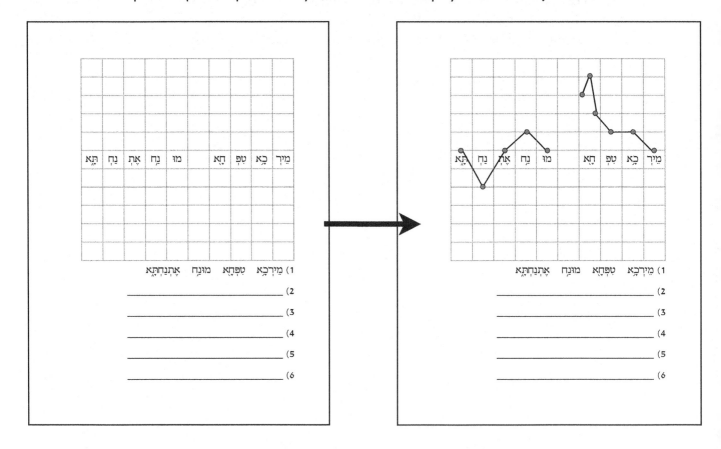

What's the point of all this trop?

Apart from musical notations, the trop (or, more properly, *te'amim*) tell us where to put the correct emphasis in each word and sentence. They also function as grammatical and syntactical notations, telling us when to pause in our reading, when to read quickly, etc. So we don't just read the punctuation — we sing it! There are seven distinct vocal systems for chanting the Tanah. Most people are familiar with Torah and Haftarah. See if you can find out what the other five are!

Section 1

1) בְּרֵאשִׁית בָּרָא אֱלֹהִים אֵ֥ת הַשָּׁמַ֖יִם

2) _____

3) _____

4) _____

5) _____

6) _____

וַיֹּ֕אמֶר אֱלֹהִ֖ים יְהִ֣י א֑וֹר וַֽיְהִי־א֗וֹר

Section 2

1) בְּרֵאשִׁית בָּרָא אֱלֹהִים הַשָּׁמַ֖יִם וְהָאָֽרֶץ

2) _____

3) _____

4) _____

5) _____

6) _____

וַיֹּ֕אמֶר אֱלֹהִ֖ים יְהִ֣י א֑וֹר וַיַּ֧רְא אֱלֹהִ֛ים

Torah Trop

(1) וַיֹּ֣אמֶר אֱלֹהִ֔ים תַּֽדְשֵׁ֤א הָאָ֙רֶץ֙ דֶּ֣שֶׁא עֵ֔שֶׂב

(2) _____

(3) _____

(4) _____

(5) _____

(6) _____

							וַ֣		
							יֹּ֣	אֶת	
							אֶ֣	תַּ֔	תָּ֤
							רֶ֔	עֵ֣	דָּ֣
							שֶׁ	אֶ֣	
							דֶּ	תַ	
							שֵׁ֤		
							וָ		
							שֵׁ֣א		

(1) וַיֹּ֣אמֶר וַיִּקָּרֵ֤א וַיַּ֖רְא הַטּֽוֹב

(2) _____

(3) _____

(4) _____

(5) _____

(6) _____

							וַ֣		
							יֹּ֣	אֶת	
							וְ	נָ֣	
							אֶ֣	רָ	
							תַ	עַ	
							הָ֤		
							רְ		
							הָ		
							וַ֥		

1) וַיֹּאמֶר יְהֹוָ֖ה   הַֽיְהֹוָ֔ה יְהֹוָ֑ה

(2) _____

(3) _____

(4) _____

(5) _____

(6) _____

וֹ   אָ֟   רִ֞   רֶ֓   הֵ֗תָ   קָ֩   רִ֞   רֶ֓

---

1) בַּיֹּ֖ום   וַיְהִ֣י־אֹ֑מֶר

(2) _____

(3) _____

(4) _____

(5) _____

(6) _____

שׁ   הַ֯   רִ֞   לֵ֟   אֵ֟ם   דַ֟   ס֯   הַ֯

Torah Trop

(1) בְּרֵאשִׁית בָּרָא אֱלֹהִים אֵת הַשָּׁמַיִם וְאֵת הָאָרֶץ

(2) _____

(3) _____

(4) _____

(5) _____

(6) _____

---

(1) בְּרֵאשִׁית אֱלֹהִים

(2) _____

(3) _____

(4) _____

(5) _____

הַשֵּׁם

הַכֹּהֵן וְאֹתָם הַכֹּהֵן לַיְהֹוָה

נֵ וַ אֶת יֵ וַ חַ סַ לַיְ

(1) _____

(2) _____

(3) _____

(4) _____

(5) _____

(6) _____

לְפָנֶי־יְהֹוָה

הָיְתָה

וְ יַ דֹוּ אַ מֵ וַ

(1) _____

(2) _____

(3) _____

(4) _____

(5) _____

(6) _____

TORAH TROP

1) אֵ֥לֶּה֩ אֵ֨לֶּה֙ וָּאֵ֔לֶּה   אֵ֥לֶּה֩ אֵ֨לֶּה֙ וָ֧אֵלֶּה

2) _____

3) _____

4) _____

5) _____

6) _____

1) אֵ֥לֶּה   אֵ֨לֶּה אֵ֧לֶּה אֵ֛לֶּה אֵ֥לֶּה אֵ֖לֶּה

2) _____

3) _____

4) _____

5) _____

6) _____

TORAH TROP

אֵ֠שׁ גֵּ֞ גֵּ֝ דֵּ֗

1) הַמִּשְׁפָּט֙ ל֖וֹט

2) _____

3) _____

4) _____

5) _____

Section 1

מֵאֵלֶּה | אֵן | עֵשׂ | אֹן | וֵיָל | אֵן | וֵוּ | וּ | לִק־

1) וְהָיָה מֵאִתְּכֶם וְהָיָה וֵיַעַקֹב־וַיֹּאמֶר

(2 _____

(3 _____

(4 _____

(5 _____

(6 _____

Section 2

וֹיֵל | אֵן | עֵשׂ | אֹן | וַל | לֵי | אֵֽרֵי | לֵי | אַלֵּי

1) וְהָיָה מֵאִתְּכֶם וַיֵּלֶךְ אֲבַרְהֵכֶם

(2 _____

(3 _____

(4 _____

(5 _____

(6 _____

1) מֵרֵאשִׁ֤ית הַמִּלְחָמָ֣ה הָאָמַ֣ר לֵאמֹ֑ר הֵשִׁ֖יב מֶ֥לֶךְ

(2 _____

(3 _____

(4 _____

(5 _____

(6 _____

			וַיֹּ֣אמֶר	זָ֣י	הֵ֖א	שֵׁ֔א	אָ֑ר	שֵׂ֤ה	שֵׁ֖	שֶׁ֥ר	זֵ֔

1) מֵרֵאשִׁ֤ית וַנֹּאמַ֣ר הַמִּלְחָמָ֣ה לְהֵיטִ֑יב

(2 _____

(3 _____

(4 _____

(5 _____

(6 _____

				אַ֥י	שֶׁ֖	רֵ֔	שֵׁ֣	זֵ֤	וַ֣	זָ֣א	שֵׁ֔א	אֵ֑ר	שֶׁ֖ה	זֵ֔

Top section

וְהָיָה   וַיְהִי   וְהָיָה   וַיְהִי

Boxed words (right to left): וְהָ אֲשֶׁ הָ הָיָ הָיָה אֲשֶׁ הָ הָיָ

1) וְהָיָה   וַיְהִי
(2 _____
(3 _____
(4 _____
(5 _____
(6 _____

Bottom section

וַיְהִי   וַיְלֶךְ־אֶל־מֶלֶךְ

Boxed words (right to left): וַיְ הִי הִ לֵ אֶל הֵ הַ מֶ

1) וַיְהִי   וַיְלֶךְ־אֶל־מֶלֶךְ
(2 _____
(3 _____
(4 _____
(5 _____
(6 _____

86

Top section

מַרְכָּא טִפְחָא – מֻנַּח אֶתְנַחְתָּא

(1) _____

(2) _____

(3) _____

(4) _____

(5) _____

(6) _____

וְ   וֵ   גֵ   אֲשֶׁ   לֵ   מֵ   רֵ   אַ

Bottom section

מַרְכָּא מְהֻפָּךְ

(1) _____

(2) _____

(3) _____

(4) _____

(5) _____

פַּשְׁטָא

שֵׁ   גֵ   מִ   שֵׁ   רֵ   מֵ   אַ

HAFTARAH TROP

HAFTARAH TROP

HAFTARAH TROP

מַ טֵ פֵּ זָ

(1

(2

(3

(4

(5

D'VAR TORAH WRITING GUIDE

This guide is intended to give you a general idea of what a typical D'var Torah looks like. Yours may not look exactly like this — it will, of course, be written by you and not me! — but it should include all of these elements. As always, make sure you consult with your rabbi / teacher.

1. Don't thank people for coming — that's something you can tell your guests at the party afterwards. The person giving the D'var Torah is called a *Darshan* — literally, an "explainer". The congregation will thank *you* for explaining the weekly readings to *them*.

2. In one or two paragraphs, summarize the content of the Torah and Haftarah readings for that day.

3. Quote a verse or idea from the Torah and/or Haftarah in Hebrew and in English, and discuss its relevance in our times. This is when you bring in your own commentaries and tell us what you've learned from our ancient and modern teachers.

4. Explain how the idea you've chosen has meaning to you. You can discuss the impact the D'var Torah may have had on how you're going to lead your life, how it's affected your commitment to Judaism and its values, etc.

5. If it fits with your ideas, you may want to talk about your parents, grandparents or other family members and role models and what positive values or lessons you've learned from them. Note: this is not the same as thanking them. Save the "thank you's" for after the service!

6. Final thoughts: what does becoming a Bar/Bat Mitzvah mean to you? Why is it special to you and what have you learned in the process of studying for today? Typically, this is where you bring your discussion back to the original idea you chose from the Torah / Haftarah.

7. Your D'var Torah should be no more than four or five double-spaced pages — roughly the length of a five to seven minute speech.

My **parashah**, book from the Torah, and chapter/verse

My **Haftarah** book and chapter/verse reference....

What the TORAH says in my own words:

What the HAFTARAH says in my own words:

Questions I have about my TORAH reading, Haftarah, Bar/Bat Mitzvah process, or Judaism in general (minimum 3):	Questions my parents have about my TORAH reading, Haftarah, Bar/Bat Mitzvah process, or Judaism in general (minimum 3):

SECTIONS OF TORAH THAT STAND OUT FOR ME...

Chapter : Verse OR Section	What it says in my own words	Why it stands out for me

SECTIONS OF HAFTARAH THAT STAND OUT FOR ME...

Chapter : Verse OR Section	What it says in my own words	Why it stands out for me

One idea or theme I want to talk about (based on my choices from charts 3 and 4):	
Verse or section from the Torah or Haftarah that relates to my theme (choose 1 or 2 from charts 3 and/or 4 and write them here):	

Commentator	The commentator's own words	What I think the commentator is trying to teach
	⬆	⬆
	⬆	⬆
	⬆	⬆

One idea or theme I want to talk about: (copy from previous chart)	
Verse or section from the Torah or Haftarah that relates to my theme: (copy from previous chart)	

Commentator (copy from previous chart)	What I think the commentator is trying to teach (copy from previous chart)	How this teaching relates to my life or the world around me
	→	→
	→	→
	→	→

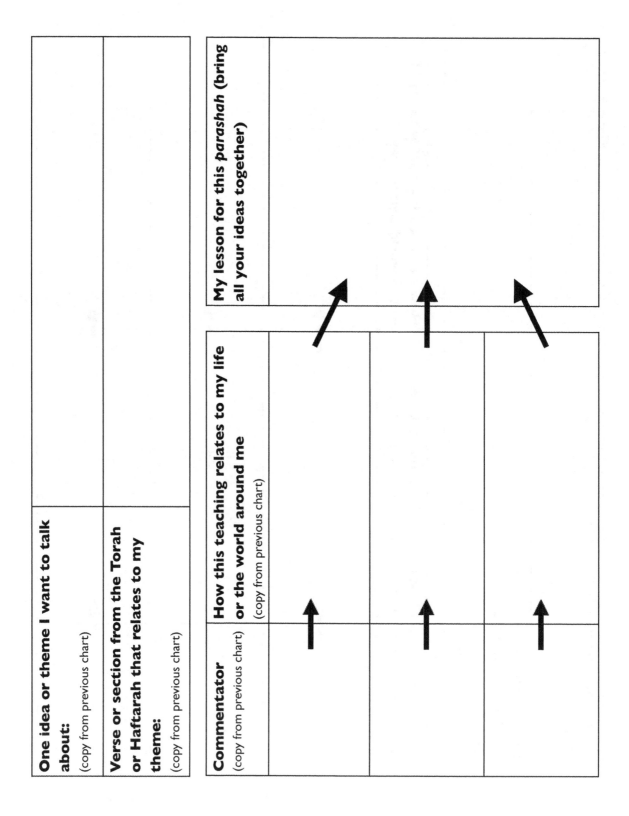

One idea or theme I want to talk about:
(copy from previous chart)

Verse or section from the Torah or Haftarah that relates to my theme:
(copy from previous chart)

Commentator
(copy from previous chart)

How this teaching relates to my life or the world around me
(copy from previous chart)

My lesson for this *parashah* (bring all your ideas together)

INCREDIBLY HANDY TIME LINE

The dates here are approximate. The two main columns compare the Tanah's chronology with samples of writings from ancient Yisra'el's neighbors that relate to events in the Tanah. There are also thousands of Hebrew inscriptions and documents dug up by archeologists, but unfortunately I don't have space to mention them all! The narrow column on the left shows you when the books of the Torah and *Nevi'im* (Prophets) take place, **not** when they were written. See if you can locate your own Torah / Haftarah readings on this time line!

WHEN TORAH BOOKS TAKE PLACE	TIME LINE FROM THE TANAH (TORAH & PROPHETS ONLY)		STUFF WRITTEN ABOUT YISRA'EL BY YISRA'EL'S NEIGHBORS
BERESHIT	First Jewish family: Avraham, Sarah, Yitzhak, Rivkah, Ya'akov, Le'ah, Rahel, Yosef and all his brothers	1600 BCE 3600 years ago	
		1500 BCE 3500 years ago	
	Benay Yisra'el in Mitzra'im	1400 BCE 3400 years ago	
		1300 BCE 3300 years ago	
SHEMOT, VAYIKRA, BAMIDBAR, DEVARIM	Time of Moshe and the Exodus	1200 BCE 3200 years ago	Egyptian Pharaoh Merneptah records a list of nations living in Cana'an. "Yisra'el" is included in the list (1205 BCE)
	Benay Yisra'el capture land of Yisra'el	years ago	

Navi Books	When Navi Books Take Place	Date	Historical Records
YEHOSHU'A, SHOFTIM	Benay Yisra'el in Mitzra'im Time of Moshe and the Exodus Benay Yisra'el capture the land of Yisra'el and settle it. Time of the *Shoftim* (tribal chiefs).	**1200 BCE** 3200 years ago **1100 BCE** 3100 years ago	Egyptian Pharaoh Merneptah records a list of nations living in Cana'an. "Yisra'el" is included in the list (1205 BCE)
SHEMU'EL, I MELAHIM	Time of King Sha'ul, King David and King Shlomo; First Temple is built; Kingdom of Yisra'el established	**1000 BCE** 3000 years ago	
	Kingdom splits into Yehudah and Yisra'el (922 BCE) Book of *1 Melahim* describes invasion of Yehudah by Pharaoh Shishak	**900 BCE** 2900 years ago	Egyptian Pharaoh Shishak writes a victory monument about invading the region in and around Yisra'el
2 MELAHIM AMOS, HOSHE'A, NAHUM, MICAH, YISH'AYAH #1	Time of Eliyahu and Elisha; Book of *2 Melahim* describes a rebellion against Yisra'el by Mesha, king of Mo'ab; *2 Melahim* also describes war between Aram, Yehudah, and Yisra'el	**800 BCE** 2800 years ago	King Mesha of Mo'ab makes a stone monument describing his rebellion against Israel; Anonymous king of Aram makes a stone monument describing war with Yehudah & Yisra'el
	Ashur conquers Yisra'el (722-720 BCE) Books of *2 Melahim* and *Yish'ayah* describe Assyrian invasions of Yehudah and Yisra'el	**700 BCE** 2700 years ago	Assyrian kings Tiglath-Pileser III and Shalmaneser V write inscriptions and wall carvings about conquering Israel; Assyrian king Sennacherib writes inscription about his invasion of Yehudah
2 MELAHIM TZEFANYAH, YIRMIYAH, YEHEZK'EL, YISH'AYAH #2, OVADYAH	**Bavel conquers Yehudah (590's-586 BCE)** Yerushalayim destroyed (586 BCE)	**600 BCE** 2600 years ago	**Babylonians write inscriptions about their invasion and conquest of Yehudah**
HAGAI, ZEHARYAH, HABAKUK, MAL'AH	Cyrus of Persia allows exiles to return from Bavel; Temple rebuilt; time of Nehemiyah & Ezra	**500 BCE** 2500 years ago	Persia conquers Babylon; Persian King Cyrus II writes inscription about his policy of allowing all exiled people to return home

WHEN *NAVI* BOOKS TAKE PLACE				
HAGAI, ZEḤARYAH, HABAKUK, MAL'AḤI	Cyrus of Persia allows exiles to return from Bavel; Temple rebuilt; time of Neḥemiyah & Ezra		**500 BCE** 2500 years ago	Persia conquers Babylon; Persian King Cyrus II writes inscription about his policy of allowing all exiled people to return home
			400 BCE 2400 years ago	
		Books of the Torah, Prophets, and other pieces of literature are edited and compiled into the Tanaḥ	**300 BCE** 2300 years ago	Greek Empire defeats Persia and takes control of the land of Israel
			200 BCE 2200 years ago	
		Jews successfully rebel against Greek Seleucid Empire & establish kingdom of Judea (Ḥanukah)	**100 BCE** 2100 years ago	
	Time of the Mishnah (final compilation roughly 200 CE)		**1 BCE / 1 CE** 2000 years ago	Dead Sea Scrolls are written and hidden in caves in the Judean Desert · Roman Empire takes control of Judea
		Jews rebel against Rome; Jerusalem and the Temple are destroyed (70 CE)	**200 CE** 1800 years ago	**Romans build a massive arch with carvings that depict the victory over the Jews**

CPSIA information can be obtained at www.ICGtesting.com
Printed in the USA
LVOW03s1726280415

436415LV00017B/561/P